PRAYER

PRAYER

Beverly LaHaye

THOMAS NELSON PUBLISHERS

NASHVILLE

Published in Nashville, Tennessee, by Thomas Nelson, Inc., and distributed in Canada by Lawson Falle, Ltd., Cambridge, Ontario.

Printed in the United States of America.

Scripture quotations are from THE NEW KING JAMES VERSION of the Bible. Copyright © 1979, 1980, 1982, Thomas Nelson, Inc., Publishers.

Library of Congress Cataloging-in-Publication Data

LaHaye, Beverly.
        Prayer / Beverly LaHaye.
            p.   cm.
        ISBN 0-8407-7464-8
        1. Prayer. I. Title.
BV220.L36   1990
248.3 '2—dc20   90–39393
                                                                 CIP

1 2 3 4 5 6 7 8 9 10 - 97 96 95 94 93 92 91 90

CONTENTS

PRAYER

CHAPTER
1

THE FINGERPRINT OF GOD

Vicki Frost is a conscientious mom who lives in the beautiful hills of Tennessee. Concerned at what she had seen in her eleven-year-old daughter's reading book, she went to the principal's office and asked to take her child out of the class. The principal called the police, and Vicki was arrested for trespassing. "I was taken to jail!" Vicki says. "The judge even threatened to take my children away from me!"

Betty Batey, a dedicated Christian, watched helplessly as her son was handed over to his homosexual father. After the father's death from AIDS, custody of the boy was awarded to the father's male lover.

Ken Roberts' problems started when he read a Bible silently in his classroom in preparation for a lesson on religions of the world. Even now, when he looks back on it, he shakes his head in disbelief. "I'm an American citizen!" he says. "How could they do this to me? I could have checked a Bible out of the school library!"

I've never been thrown in jail. I've never had to watch helplessly as my children were torn away

11

from me. I've never had my job threatened because I would not set aside my Christian principles. Yet I have something in common with Vicki and Betty and Ken. I, too, have run up against things I was helpless to handle. Terrifying things. Painful, frustrating things. Like Vicki, Betty, and Ken, and millions of others around the world, I have been brought to a place where there was nothing to do but fall on my face before the Lord.

"I really believe it was the prayers of an awful lot of people that kept me from being wiped out a long time ago," says Ken.

Evelyn Smith, a California widow who was prosecuted for not wanting to rent her apartment to an unmarried couple, knows what Ken means. "I have a lot of friends who prayed for me," she says. "But it's all those people I don't even know who write and tell me they are praying for me who give me so much strength. Just imagine! They don't even know me, yet they take the time to write and tell me they care."

Evelyn Smith knew she couldn't simply drop her case. "God wouldn't want me to do that," she insisted. Yet attorneys are so expensive. In desperation, she contacted our attorneys at Concerned Women for America. "CWA was sent by God," Mrs. Smith says.

When we pray, we immediately start looking for answers to our prayers. But how exciting it is to *be* the answer to someone else's prayer! That's one of the reasons I am so proud and honored to be the president of Concerned Women for America. With a small group of ladies, I founded CWA in San Diego, California, in 1979. From that humble beginning, we have grown to represent over 700,000 households in America, and that makes us the largest women's organization in the United States.

Not too many years ago, I would never have dreamed of being in such a position. I was just a shy, fearful wife of a pastor. Certainly, I was concerned about our country, and especially about anything that directly affected our congregation and my family. But speak out? Never! It was hard enough for me to bring myself to pray aloud in church. Yet so much has happened in these past several years that I could never go back to what I once was.

THE POWER OF PRAYER

Everything I'm doing today is a tribute to the power of prayer. Let me tell you an incident from my life that might illustrate why prayer is so important to me.

Twenty years ago, I had a minor automobile accident that pulled my arm out of the socket. It slipped right back in after a few minutes of excruciating pain, but overnight I was stricken with rheumatoid arthritis. From that day on, the crippling disease grew worse and worse. Since the day of that accident, I've hardly been without pain.

For about two or three years after its onset, the arthritis became increasingly severe. Finally, I couldn't hold a pencil in my hand. I couldn't write a letter or sign my name on a check.

Now I was still a young woman. I had children at home and a husband busy in the ministry. They needed me. There was so much I wanted to do, so much to accomplish. Yet simple, everyday routines such as combing my own hair and putting on lipstick were becoming impossible. My hands often were frozen into claws and getting more and more useless by the day.

I went for an intensive two weeks of testing at Scripps Clinic near our home in San Diego. What the doctors had to say plunged me into even greater depths of despair. I was told to take 16–18 aspirin each day and within the next couple of years I would probably be confined to a wheelchair.

Depression overwhelmed me. It seemed like my life was as good as over. I tried hard to refuse to believe my condition would really deteriorate so far, but the evidence was there. Besides my deformed hands, I was having to contend with feet that no longer worked properly. Already my toes were starting to curl up, and every step was racked with pain.

At the doctors' suggestion, I began attending classes to learn how to care for myself. Painfully, slowly, I remastered skills I had once performed without a second thought. I learned how to use my stiff, claw-shaped fingers to pick up a cup. Doorknobs were especially hard. With fingers that wouldn't bend, I struggled and struggled to learn to turn knobs. Though I could still walk, I practiced maneuvering myself around in a wheelchair for hours. "You must do it," the doctors told me. "It's only a matter of time."

I plunged into such a deep fog of depression that I didn't see what was happening to me. Fortunately, my husband, Tim, became alarmed at what he saw. And the 18 aspirin each day began to affect my personality. "You're being programmed to be a cripple!" he told me.

So my dear husband took me aside and said, "You must stop picturing yourself in a wheelchair. By seeing yourself that way, you're just giving in to it. I don't believe that's what God has for you in the future."

Tim had more faith than I had.

Without a doubt, this was the lowest period of my life. I call it my black year. I went through an unbelievable depression. Pain racked by body from head to toe. Every morning, I awoke to find that a different part of me wouldn't work right. I was so crippled up and in such pain that I could no longer care for myself. Instead of my taking care of my husband and children as I had always done, my family was now caring for me. How I hated it!

One morning, I struggled and struggled before I managed to make my painful way out of bed and to the kitchen. No longer could I pour my own coffee. My daughter handed me the cup, and it was all I could do to pick it up and lift it to my mouth. I was rapidly losing the ability to do even the simplest things for myself. From the depths of my terrible depression I cried out, *Is this what the rest of my life is going to be like?* It was not a prayer, just a silent cry of misery and anguish.

In those horrible days, my depression and frustration were so deep and so black that I got to where I couldn't even pray. But Tim could. He took over praying for me when I couldn't pray for myself. Day after day, week after week, month after month, Tim spent hours pleading with God on my behalf.

As he prayed, Tim encouraged me to try

every kind of treatment possible. I wore copper brace-lets. I went to Mexico for a special treatment. I went to a spa in Palm Springs where the waters were said to have healing properties. Nothing helped. Not one thing I tried made a single bit of difference.

And yet Tim wouldn't give up. He kept praying, he kept encouraging, and he kept searching for an answer.

At the doctor's suggestion, I acquired a wax-melting machine to use at home. Every morning it became my ritual to come down to the kitchen and dip my hands in and out, in and out, of very, very hot wax, as hot as I could handle it. I kept this up until I had a thick coat of wax on each hand. Then I wrapped my hands in foil, then the foil in a towel. For thirty minutes I sat while that heat penetrated to the very marrow of my aching bones. It felt wonderful! When the thirty minutes were over, I peeled the wax off. For a few hours my hands felt better, and I had more movement in them. But by evening the effects had worn off, and I was right back where I started.

In those dark days, I sat by my stereo and listened to the Gaithers' musical *Alleluia* again and again and again. With tears running down my face I'd think, *I want to be able to say, "Alleluia." I want to say, "Praise the Lord" and really mean it. But how can I?* I couldn't even pray for myself.

After several years, Tim read about a treat-ment in Romania called Gerovital that had shown suc-cess in cases like mine. So he flew with me and I enrolled in a clinic for two weeks of treatment. It was there in Romania that I finally began to see a ray of hope. Of all the treatments I had tried, here at last was one that actually slowed down my disease's progression. I wasn't healed, but I was no longer getting worse.

Although the Romanian treatment and medication were a great medical help, I know full well that it was God Himself who stopped the progress of my arthritis. And it is God who since that time has brought me so far. God heard my husband's prayers, and He answered them in a miraculous way. Not only am I not in a wheelchair, but I am also more active than I have ever been in my life. I turn doorknobs with fingers that bend. I comb my own hair and put on lipstick. I even open most jars without help. For me, every day is a reason for praise and thanksgiving.

People who hear my story often ask, "Why didn't you ask God to *heal* you?" Well, I *did* ask! In fact, I *begged* God for healing. Not only Tim, but people all over the country were praying for me. I did everything I could think of to convince God to remove the disease from my body completely. I attended many healing meetings.

But God chose *not* to heal me, at least not in the instantaneous way I had in mind. What I see Him doing is healing me in a gradual way. Me, in a wheelchair? Hardly! Today I hike through the Costa Rican jungle to work with Nicaraguan refugees in places I never before would have attempted. Struggle with jars and doorknobs? Very seldom! Now I use my hands to do things I'd never before attempted. Not only can I now *comb* my own hair, I totally *do* my own hair. I haven't time to go to a beauty shop! I've had to learn to do it, and I'm able to accomplish it without a great struggle now that my hands are working more normally.

Oh, I still have pain. Some mornings I wake up with a totally new ache. Since arthritis moves around the body, I'm never quite sure where it will strike next. Sometimes it's a shoulder, other times it's a knee or a hand. In my hands and feet I still carry the marks of the disease. I still take the Romanian medication regularly. And my husband still prays for me. When I'm having a specific pain, Tim will pray for that particular pain. "Lord," he will say, "Beverly has so much to do today. She has hands to shake, and her hand is hurting. Help that hand to be strong today." And God answers Tim's prayers.

I pray for myself too, and many of my prayers are prayers of thanksgiving because I have so much to be thankful for. For although I haven't seen an end to my disease, what a miraculous answer to prayer I have seen!

So, you see, I know what it means to fight an ongoing battle. And although it is sometimes hard to recognize, there is a special blessing in that kind of a struggle, for those ongoing battles allow for ongoing victories. No, God didn't heal me completely. But He gives me enough use of my body to do what He wants me to do today. My physical condition has been a constant reminder to me that I need God's help every day.

Discouragement? Yes, I know what that is too. More than once I've cried out to God, "Lord, You've given me this calling, but You haven't given me the body to do what You called me to do. I don't understand it!" I've had speaking engagements when I've been in so much pain I didn't see how I could possibly meet my commitment. I packed myself up and struggled aboard the plane, not knowing how I could ever minister to anyone. Yet when I got to my destination, the hurting was gone. Instead of my facial expression being tense with pain, I smiled. I stood and walked sufficiently to do what I needed to do. I shook hands.

All weekend I ministered comfortably. Then I headed back home and—guess what? Monday morning I was hurting again. It was almost as if God was teaching me yet another lesson: "Beverly, you do what I've called you to do and let me take care of your body." Even on those days when I wasn't sure I could manage to lift my suitcases and board the plane, I kept doing what I was convinced God wanted me to do. And each time it was a little easier and a little less painful.

As God continued to widen the scope of my ministry to what it is today, He has continued to give me just enough strength and relief from pain to do what I need to do. I call that a healing. Not the healing that my human reason expected, but a healing that God totally controls.

In this book we're going to look at the subject of prayer through the eyes of ordinary people who have found themselves thrust into extraordinary circumstances, people who have learned firsthand the power of prayer. When they are asked, "Yes, but does prayer *really* work?" they know what to say, and they can tell you why. We're going to look at some powerful principles of prayer and offer specific suggestions you can apply to improve your own prayer life. We're going to show you people who dared to speak boldly and "put feet to their prayers." But we're not going to stop there. We're also going to challenge you to be a woman or man who cares—*really* cares.

Vicki Frost and Betty Batey and Ken Roberts and Evelyn Smith and Beverly LaHaye are only some of the people who have learned what it means to pray—really to pray—when everything depends on God's answer.

Prayer, I believe, is God's protection for ourselves and our families, a strategic weapon to save our children. Prayer is the fingerprint of God upon our lives.

Do you know the power of God in your life? Have you seen miraculous answers to your prayers? Would you like to? Then come along and meet some of those who can show you what can happen when you pray.

CHAPTER
2

DOES PRAYER REALLY MAKE A DIFFERENCE?

W hen CWA attorney Jordan Lorence went home to Minnesota for Christmas in 1988, he had no idea he was about to become an answer to prayer.

At a Christmas party another attorney happened to mention, "I just got a call from a Reverend James Bzoskie. He's the pastor of a little church over in the town of Hastings."

The city of Hastings had ordered the church to vacate a downtown storefront property it had rented for a number of years, the attorney told Jordan. "The area is zoned for commercial activity," they said, "not religious worship. Bzoskie has tried for two years to get the city to change this zoning ordinance so he could remain in the storefront. Because of his small congregation of only one hundred people, he cannot afford a location in Hastings that is zoned for religious worship."

Despite Pastor Bzoskie and church members' attempts to work the problem out with the city and although they had attended meeting after meeting, they were finally given a deadline: they had to be out of their building by January 1.

"No way can that little church afford a court battle," the attorney told Jordan. Then he added, "Isn't it sad that churches have so few rights?"

That set Jordan to thinking. The next day he called up Pastor Bzoskie and introduced himself as an attorney with Concerned Women for America. Then he asked, "May I come over tomorrow and go over your case with you?"

Pastor Bzoskie could hardly speak! An attorney from Washington, D.C., was coming to *him* and offering to help without charging! He had been praying so hard, and now out of the blue, God was offering him an answer far beyond anything he ever dared expect.

"We had come to the end of everything we could do," Charlotte Bzoskie said. "We were certain God heard our prayers, yet at times we cried out in frustration, 'Lord, *what* is going on?' We were under so much pressure."

Charlotte's mother had just broken her leg, and Charlotte was spending a lot of time running between her house and her mother's.

"Every time I saw Mom, she asked, 'How's it going with the church?' And I'd say, 'Not so good. We can't even afford a lawyer.' Mom would say, 'You know, God could send you the help you need.' And I'd answer, 'Well, I know He can if that's what He wants.' But I never really expected it to happen."

Sometimes the Bzoskies felt so low, they prayed, "Lord, maybe this isn't what You want after all." Yet they were certain God *did* want their church to stay right where it was.

"What we didn't know was what we could do to keep it there," Charlotte said.

The uncertainty was especially hard for Pastor Bzoskie. "I'm a doer by nature," he told me. "I want to keep things moving."

Finally, on a cold winter morning in late December, Pastor Jim and Charlotte Bzoskie sat together in the kitchen of their home. They had come to the end of everything within their power. That day they determined they were going to be obedient to God's call to preach even if it meant setting up orange crates in the middle of the street. Together, at their kitchen table, they prayed.

"We just totally gave the problem to God that day," Pastor Bzoskie said. "I had every intention that, come January, we would bring the congregation to our house."

Prayer first. Then action. That's been the bedrock of my life, and that's the cornerstone of Concerned Women for America. I believe that prayer is important before we act. If we act in our own strength, then we'll walk in our own strength. But when we pray and then act, we walk in God's strength.

WALKING IN GOD'S STRENGTH

What happens when we walk in God's strength?

Ask Moses. He'll tell you that those who walk in God's strength can command the waters to part so that they can walk through the Red Sea.

Or ask David. That little shepherd boy killed

the giant Goliath, who was probably six feet taller than David and hundreds of pounds heavier.

Or ask the apostle Paul. He traveled many miles through storms at sea, suffered beatings, was imprisoned in terrible conditions, and was still able to write, "I have learned in whatever state I am, to be content" (Phil. 4:11).

The list goes on and on. It begins with the biblical heroes of long ago and continues today with Christians like Pastor Jim Bzoskie.

"We pray," Pastor Bzoskie said, "because we want God's fingerprints on everything that happens, and we want none of our own. That way, it is God who gets the glory."

And so Pastor Bzoskie prayed. The very next morning Jordan Lorence called.

"I had absolutely nothing to do with it," Pastor Bzoskie insisted. "We'd given the problem over to God. Then out of the blue, an attorney from Washington calls and says, 'I'd like to come and visit you. Could you give me some time?' I knew immediately it was from God!"

As Jordan Lorence was leaving, Pastor Bzoskie told him, "Whether you take our case or not, you have done more to build us up than you will ever know. God answered our prayers! Someone has taken the time to listen to us!"

Then, right after Jordan left, Charlotte Bzoskie called her mother. "God really did it!" she said.

Her mother wasn't surprised. "See? I told you God can bring things out of nowhere!"

"We hadn't even asked for anything like

that," Charlotte Bzoskie insisted. "God brought that attorney right here to us. It was pretty amazing, all right." Then she added, "We always knew God would answer our prayers, but He answered in a way we never even dreamed of. It was a far better answer than we had in mind."

When Jordan came back to Washington and explained the plight of Cornerstone Bible Church, I agreed we should take the case, but only after I had sought the Lord's leading in this critical situation.

To this day Pastor Bzoskie insists it was a miracle.

"You always hear about miracles happening to somebody else," he says, "but one happened right here to little Cornerstone Bible Church in the small town of Hastings, Minnesota. It just shows that God does have purposes for His people, no matter who or where we are!"

It's exciting to hear such answers to prayer. But other times we seem to pray and pray about a concern, yet nothing happens. Many people have said to me, "I don't think God even hears my prayers. Does He really hear us when we pray?" This is the first of a trio of questions that keep many people from walking in God's strength.

DOES GOD HEAR OUR PRAYERS?

I know exactly how people feel when they ask such questions. I've been there. The secret is to keep on praying. When we feel it's doing no good, we need to keep on praying. When we no longer feel like praying,

27

we should do it anyway. When we get discouraged and frustrated, we need to keep on praying for faith that God will bring that answer in the right time and in the right way.

"It was that morning when Charlotte and I bowed before God in our kitchen, just days before our church had to move, that we finally let go of the problem," said Pastor Bzoskie. "Finally God was free to work. Sometimes we want God in the situation, but we want to be in it too. We want to have our fingerprints on the outcome. We need to come to the place where we say, 'God, we want Your fingerprints on everything that happens here, and we want none of ours.'"

Pastor Bzoskie is convinced that people of prayer are the unsung heroes in the Christian church, that theirs is the most powerful place to be. "When we get to heaven," he says, "and God says, 'Okay, it's time for rewards,' He's going to call some senior citizen who has been a prayer warrior and say, 'Come here, Sister.' How surprised we will be to find it was that grandma's prayers that were the building blocks and foundation stones for all the miracles we saw and thought we had brought about!"

Does God hear our prayers? Without doubt.

Once this first question is answered, the next natural question is: "If God hears our prayers, then why doesn't He answer them?"

DOES GOD ANSWER PRAYER?

If I didn't believe with all my heart that God truly does answer prayer, my life as I am presently living it would come to an abrupt halt. This work I do, the people with whom I must mix, the intense situations in which I find myself involved—I couldn't handle them. Let me give you an example.

I am often asked to appear on talk shows. The first time I was on "Donahue" was in the spring of 1982, six months before Ronald Reagan was elected president the first time. I was asked to bring along two other women from Concerned Women for America.

The one thing that made me a bit wary was that Phil Donahue had let us fill up the entire studio with CWA people from the Chicago area. The three of us were very comfortable up there on the stage. We were among friends, just talking and explaining our organization. It wasn't usual for Phil Donahue to allow such a homogeneous audience. I had the feeling that something wasn't quite right, yet I just couldn't get a handle on the problem.

In his friendly way, Phil Donahue talked with us about CWA. Then about midway through the program he asked, "Now, you're all Republicans aren't you?" We hedged, for legally we cannot be a partisan group.

He pressed harder. "Is anyone here *not* for Reagan?" he asked the studio audience. Then in an expert way, he proceeded to twist the political question all around.

Suddenly he switched tactics. "Are all of you Christians?" he asked the audience. Then he proceeded to twist *that* all around.

In summary Phil said, "So, to be a Christian you have to be a Reagan supporter. Is that right?" He was really setting the stage for something that looked like it was going to be ugly. But that's all he did with it. He didn't carry it any further.

When the show was all over, I thought, *This is really strange. It's not even a good show. Why would Phil Donahue put together something like this?*

Two weeks later we got a call from a prayer chapter leader in Chicago. "We just got a call from Phil Donahue's office saying they want ten of our ladies to be on a program," she said. "They only want us to fill ten chairs. They'll take care of the rest of the audience."

I told her, "We'd better handpick those ten, because that man is really going to blast you."

We carefully chose ten women, but at the last minute a couple of ladies were not able to be on the show. We had to use substitutes who were not nearly as informed or used to public speaking. The program went on, and, sure enough, Donahue had an ACLU attorney, someone from People for the American Way, and someone from the National Organization for Women. Needless to say, none of those people were on our side.

First, a clip of the program from two weeks before was shown. Then, the panel started blasting it, and I mean hard. Now, because of our tax status, we cannot be partisan. We must be politically neutral. Phil Donahue set out to prove that to be part of our organization, one must be a Christian Republican. Despite our efforts to prove that assumption wrong, he would not give up.

Next, Donahue went out into the audience with his microphone. Would you believe it? He immediately spotted our weakest link and headed right for her.

Phil Donahue jammed that microphone right in her face and demanded, "Are you a Christian?"

Very confidently and proudly the dear lady said, "Yes."

"Are you a member of CWA?"

"Yes, I am," she answered.

"Are you a Republican?"

"Yes."

"Do you believe you have to be a Christian to go to heaven?"

"Yes, I do," she said. Even then, she had no idea she was falling right into Phil Donahue's trap.

"Jews don't believe in Jesus. Do you think Jews will go to heaven?" he asked.

"Well, uh, I don't . . . I mean, not unless . . . unless . . ." She had no answer.

Donahue continued to fire question after question, all the while putting words into her mouth. The poor woman was no match for him. He treated her as though she were on the witness stand. In the end, Phil Donahue managed to turn the whole thing around to suggest that Concerned Women for America was anti-Semitic. It was one of the ugliest, most vicious distortions I have ever witnessed.

When the microphone was turned back to the group on the stage they all agreed that, yes, CWA definitely was anti-Semitic. We didn't even get a chance to offer a rebuttal.

That day I made a decision: never again would I want any of our CWA people on "Donahue." He's too unfair.

Does God answer prayer?

We had alerted our prayer chapters to pray for the show, and they did. Yet it certainly didn't go as we would have wished. We learned an important lesson here: *The fact that we pray about something doesn't mean it will go smoothly and easily and totally our way.*

When things don't work out the way we think best, it doesn't mean we didn't pray. Nor does it mean we didn't pray enough or that we didn't pray correctly. It is our job to be faithful, to pray, and to trust God. That's where our job ends. Providing the right answer and the correct timing are God's jobs.

We who trust God are in a war. And I guarantee you, we are not going to win every battle. But we do have the advantage of knowing how the war will end because we have the Book and we've read the last chapter. Yet on our way to that last chapter, we're bound to lose some battles.

"Donahue" was one of the lost battles. Still, God was in control. We did what we could. We went down to the studio and we stood for righteousness. That's all God asked of us. We were not responsible for the fact that Donahue twisted and perverted our message.

That's not the end of the Donahue story, however. After the program aired, we started getting letters from people who saw it and were furious at Phil Donahue. He did himself no good. We gained many friends as a result of that show.

We doubt the power of prayer most when we try to predetermine how God should answer.

SOMETIMES THE ANSWER IS UNEXPECTED

Pastor Bzoskie said, "God gave Charlotte and me an answer to our prayers far beyond anything we ever expected." When God responds in a way that seems miraculous, we recognize His answer, even though it's different from what we were looking for. But when God seems silent or things go against us rather than for us, we don't think God has answered at all.

Yet very often God chooses to answer our prayers in other ways than we have in mind. For instance, we at CWA were convinced Judge Robert Bork was the best nomination for President Reagan for the Supreme Court of the United States. There was no doubt in our minds he was the right man at the right time.

We were praying for his confirmation, and we were seeing answers to our prayers. The very fact that I was allowed to testify at his hearing was in itself an answer to prayer. Usually conservatives find the door slammed shut when they request an opportunity to testify.

The appointment was to come up for a vote right after our Concerned Women for America national convention in Washington, D.C., an event attended by more than two thousand CWA members. At the convention we gave a report on Bork's nomination and the hearing, then we asked everyone to pray and pray and pray some more. That day, two thousand CWA members united in prayer for the Bork appointment.

Some women, determined to do even more, decided to make signs. They got poster board and pens;

then that evening they went to work. The next day they went out and demonstrated in front of the Senate building where the voting was to take place. It was done properly and with dignity, yet those women certainly made their point.

The next day President Reagan spoke to our convention. When he walked into the room, the whole place just exploded. He looked out at the cheering women and men and said, "I feel like the reinforcements have just arrived!"

The next week Judge Robert Bork's nomination was turned down. What a devastating disappointment! We had worked so hard and had prayed so much! We just couldn't understand it. Why had God not answered our prayers?

But do you know what? Since that disappointing defeat Judge Bork has done our country so much good. He is able to speak openly and freely, something he could not have done were he a member of the Supreme Court. His book, *Battle for Justice,* was on the *New York Times* bestseller list for many months in late 1989 and early 1990. Hundreds of thousands of Americans read about the struggles during his confirmation process and about his opinions on abortion and other critical issues. He speaks and lectures throughout the country as only he can do in his present position as a qualified man who ran well and lost.

Who knows how many Americans have changed their opinions about the confirmation process for Supreme Court justices or about critical issues such as abortion from reading this book? Not too long ago an evangelical theologian named Francis Schaeffer wrote many books exposing the humanistic trend of our society. People like Jerry Falwell and Randall Terry of Operation Rescue read those books. So did Tim and I. Our work is his work, his legacy to America. As Schaeffer said, "Once an idea has been unleashed, no one can stop its impact." Only God knows if one of the people who read *Battle for Justice* might someday be a judge or a congressional representative or the president of the United States. People prayed for Judge Bork and God answered—just a little differently than we all expected.

Even that's not the end of the story. After Judge Bork's defeat, God brought along Justice Scalia, a young man who will be on the bench of the Supreme Court for years, God willing. So all is far from lost. Certainly we would have loved to see Judge Bork seated on the Supreme Court. But God knows best. We *think* we know. Sometimes we are *certain* we know. But in the end only God really knows.

Here's a little postscript. The year after his defeat, we invited Judge Bork to our convention, since we knew he was a great American who still had the opportunity to have an enormous impact on America. Because our women all across the country had been praying for him by name, they felt as if he were a personal friend. Besides, so much of what he stands for represents what is in our own hearts.

He accepted our invitation and, along with his wife and son, attended our convention. He rarely takes a meeting like that, he told us, but in this case he felt he wanted to be with this group that had supported his nomination very enthusiastically.

When Judge Bork came forward to address our convention, our women gave him a standing ovation. We thought we would never get them to quiet down! First we showed a clip of President Reagan from the year before, saying so many very fine things about Judge Bork. And Judge Bork, this great man, sat there on the platform with tears running down his face. After all he'd gone through—that hearing with all its misrepresentations and unfair attacks, all the things the press had said about him, all the tearing apart he had endured—through it all he never had heard the President say all those supportive things about him. And when he saw that tape, he just could not hold back the emotion.

When I introduced Judge Bork to the audience, this great man was so choked up he could hardly speak. I presented him with the gavel we thought he should have. We had had his name engraved on it.

Without a doubt, God had a perfect reason for not permitting Judge Bork to be a part of the Supreme Court. We certainly trust His superior wisdom. Yet we wanted that man to know we never stopped supporting him. I am convinced God is going to use Judge Bork to open the eyes of many college students, attorneys, and leaders. After all, the prayers of hundreds and hundreds of women are behind him. Wherever he speaks, women come up to him and say, "I've been praying for you."

Does God answer prayer? He certainly does! Though not always according to our plans.

The final question of this typical trio of questions is: If God hears my prayers and if He answers them, then does that answer really make a difference?

DOES PRAYER REALLY MAKE A DIFFERENCE?

Does prayer really make a difference, or is it just a formality Christians go through? I'm often asked this question and I've asked it myself. If you're honest, I'm sure most of you will admit to having asked it, too. It's a legitimate question. The *Humanist Manifesto* states that prayer is simply a crutch for Christians. Is it possible the secular humanists know something we don't know? Let's consider the evidence.

At Concerned Women for America we get many, many requests for legal help. We pray about each one and trust God to show us whether or not we are to get involved. We do have guidelines, of course, but in the end we have to trust in God's wisdom. Sometimes we take a case and proceed to win everything right down the line. What a great feeling! When that happens, we feel we are certainly in the center of God's will.

But there are other cases that don't progress so smoothly or end so positively. Does that mean we aren't in God's will on those? Not at all! I don't believe that the more we pray, the more cases we will win. If I did, whenever we lost a case, I'd have to take it to mean we failed to pray enough. The fact is that we can pray and pray some more, and sometimes God still allows us to lose a case. We don't know why. Sometimes we may never know why. But God is sovereign, and we know He is at work.

The skilled attorneys at CWA spend a great deal of time and effort preparing for each trial. They also take time to pray over each and every case. Yet we know by experience that, regardless of the skill of the attorneys, regardless of the time and effort they invest, it is God alone who determines the outcome.

Once we made the decision to represent the Cornerstone Bible Church, Jordan Lorence immediately filed in federal court, and the city of Hastings agreed to let the church stay in the building until the case could be settled.

We believe the city's ordinance restricts religious activity in a way that violates the Constitution. The lawsuit notes that the city permits the Masonic lodge to locate in the commercial zone. "The Masons engage in religious-type activity, and they are a private club. Why can the Masons locate in that area but not a church?" our attorney asks. Other First Amendment activities, such as counseling centers and dance studios can permissibly locate in the commercial zone.

The city argues that churches have a negative effect on commercial activity when they are located near stores. Jordan Lorence disputes that claim, saying it lacks foundation because many towns and cities have churches located next to stores.

"There is nothing about churches that poisons commercial trade. The Supreme Court has said that the city must have a commercial trade. The Supreme Court has said that the city must have a compelling state interest to justify its burden on the church's First Amendment right to meet for worship," Jordan contends.

Ironically, courts have restricted the ability of cities to regulate the location of pornography stores with their zoning ordinances. "I think we will win this case. It would be odd indeed if the Constitution protects pornography stores from zoning ordinances but not churches," says Jordan.

A victory in this case could help new churches with limited finances for renting space. A win could also help churches and Christian schools to avoid obstacles created by overly broad zoning ordinances. The final lines just may be written in the Supreme Court of the United States. Pastor Bzoskie is willing to follow it that far.

"Imagine!" he says. "It just may be that our little church will be able to be of help to other Christians in other churches all across the country!"

The amassed, combined prayers of thousands of concerned Christians throughout America shook the gates of heaven on Bork's behalf. As CWA president, I testified at the Bork nomination hearings. A small group of middle Americans, led by a determined pastor, appealed to God in a small town in Minnesota. Then that pastor and a CWA attorney filed a lawsuit contesting the city's zoning ordinance. And one small voice prayed a simple prayer in an isolated Latin American jungle. And miraculously, miles away in America, CWA heard that prayer and acted.

THE ANSWER TO ONE SMALL CRY

While in Costa Rica distributing food and clothes to Nicaraguan refugees, we heard the cry again and again that families were cold at night and had no way to find blankets for warmth. We see so many desperate needs among the poverty-stricken refugees down there that it's hard to decide which ones we should tackle. Yet on my flight back home, I just couldn't get the picture of those shivering little children out of my mind. A few days later, I visited my own grandchildren and saw them snugly wrapped in their warm blankets each night. This tugged at my heart until I finally prayed, "Lord, what can I do?"

Over the next few weeks, wherever I spoke I shared the cry of the refugees for their need of blankets for the children. God opened the hearts of many during that time. People started giving me $5, $10, and one group even took a love offering for blankets. What a blessing! On my very next trip to Costa Rica, I took the "blanket" money with me and told Jim Woodall, our director in charge of refugee humanitarian aid, "Buy as many blankets as this money will buy. I am going to stay until every blanket is handed out." The Lord had answered my prayers of "Lord, what can I do?" He clearly showed us and we did just as He directed.

With the blankets piled in the back of the truck, Jim took me out to see some of the groups of refugees trying to find refuge along the northern border of Costa Rica. We traveled for miles along every kind of road and path until we came to a cluster of huts. We stopped at one little grass hut where an eighty-two-year-old woman named Juanita lived with her family.

Juanita had walked for three months just to get out of Nicaragua. She arrived with only what she could carry on her back. The cataracts on her eyes were so bad she could hardly see, and her body ached with arthritis. Her bed was a wooden pallet in the corner of a little shack that she shared with nine other family members. The jungle nights were cold and she shivered because their blankets had to be left behind. So she started praying for one. Even as she had prayed each day and night for safety as they trudged for three months to escape the terror of the Sandinistas, she now prayed for God's provision for her bodily warmth.

Her daughter didn't have Juanita's faith. "Nobody cares about us!" she told her mother. "Where in the world do you think you're going to get a blanket?"

Still Juanita prayed.

"We haven't got anything," her daughter said. "We're way out here in the middle of the jungle. You are not going to get a blanket, so you might as well stop praying for it."

And then Jim and I walked into the hut. When I saw Juanita's little frail body sitting on a little wooden stool, I walked over and wrapped a blanket around her. She looked at me as though I had just dropped out of heaven. Then she turned to her daughter and said matter-of-factly, "See? God heard my prayer. I knew he would bring me a blanket."

Does God answer prayer? Ask Juanita.

You'll find her in the jungles on the Costa Rican border wrapped in a warm blanket. Her prayers did not cease after a day or two. She continued to ask and trust God to meet her needs. He did and will continue to do so.

As you go through life, there will surely be times you'll be perplexed by a "no" or a "not yet" answer from God. Though you are certain your request is within God's will, the answer just doesn't come. When this happens, step back, let go, and leave the problem in God's hands. Tell Him that although you don't understand, you do trust Him. Keep praying, but while you wait for the answer, move ahead knowing *He* is Lord.

"It seems like every corner we've turned, there's been more opposition," Pastor Bzoskie says, "but today I'm more encouraged to pray than ever before, because I know—I know for certain—that God does answer prayer!"

Prayer, you see, is more than just an avenue for petitions to be made before God. Prayer is more than just a wish list. Prayer is coming into the presence of God. It is a wise person who recognizes his need for God in the midst of *all* his affairs.

When you pray, *ask for God's answer,* not yours. His answer will always be best. In Jeremiah 29:11 we read: "For I know the thoughts that I think toward you . . . thoughts of peace and not of evil, to give you a future and a hope."

Pray for God's timing, not yours. His timing, too, will always be best. According to Hebrews 4:16, "Let us therefore come boldly to the throne of grace, that we may obtain mercy and find grace to help in time of need." The Amplified Bible says it this way: "well-timed help, coming just when we need it."

Does God answer prayer? We know He does. When His children pray, God answers. Not some of their prayers. Not most of their prayers. No, God answers *all* of their prayers—*in His way and in His time*.

The right answer at the right time. That's God's way.

CHAPTER
3

TEACH ME
TO PRAY

I'm an American citizen! They can't do this to me!" Ken Roberts exclaimed.

Mr. Roberts' crime? He checked a Bible out of the school library, and occasionally read it silently in his classroom during a fifteen minute silent reading time he held daily for his students.

Ken Roberts is a fifth-grade school teacher at an elementary school outside of Denver, Colorado. During his eighteen years of teaching, his only intention was to be a good, responsible instructor to his students. But when the principal confronted him about the Bible unobtrusively tucked away on his desk and two Christian books in his classroom library, she insisted he was violating the Constitution.

Mr. Roberts had 239 books on the shelves of his classroom library, books on practically every subject imaginable. His collection included such titles as *Charlotte's Web, The Wizard of Oz, Tom Sawyer,* and *A Tale of Two Cities.* If the kids didn't bring a book from home, they were free to choose whatever appealed to them from the classroom library. Of all those 239 books, only two were of a Christian nature: *The Story of Jesus* and *The Bible in Pictures*. Neither book stood out. They were older editions, illustrated with old black and white pen drawings. Nothing flashy about them.

During the class's daily fifteen-minute silent reading time, Mr. Roberts set an example for the kids by reading at his desk. Occasionally he read from the Bible he kept on his desk.

Shortly after school started in September 1987, a parent noticed the two Christian books in Mr. Roberts' library. She complained to the principal. Immediately the principal went to Mr. Roberts' room and ordered him to remove the books.

He complied.

Then she told him to hide his copy of the Bible inside a drawer. "Students might see it and want to read it and then might accept its idea," she reasoned.

Ken Roberts still finds the whole thing bewildering. "I could have checked that Bible out of the school library!" he says emphatically. "Yet I can't read it in my classroom. What sense does that make?"

Evidently the principal didn't know anything about the school library containing a Bible. When she heard about it in a casual conversation with another teacher and the school librarian, she insisted that it, too, had to go. She told the librarian to remove it from one of the shelves for special reference books. The library books on Buddhism, and American Indian religions could stay, both in the school library and Roberts' classroom library.

Shortly after his confrontation with the

principal, Ken Roberts was giving a lecture to his students on American Indian culture. The principal dropped in just as he was holding up an Indian blanket and explaining how it depicted Navajo Indians praying to the rainbow goddess for a good harvest. She said nothing.

Later, in the teachers' lounge, Ken Roberts asked the principal if there was any problem with his mentioning that the Indians prayed to their goddess.

"That's fine," the principal said. "The Indians prayed to a rainbow goddess, not to Jesus."

So much for the separation of church and state!

Ken Roberts prayed a lot about his situation. "But I didn't feel like I was getting any answer," he says. Then he started reading the Bible. "One verse really jumped out at me. It was where Paul asked his attackers, 'What are you doing with me? I'm a Roman citizen.' With that, his attackers backed off. Well, I'm an American citizen. When my attackers realized what they were doing, surely, I figured, they too would back off."

But they didn't. This is America, but as Ken Roberts quickly learned, even in our country Christians meet with prejudice.

"Before we went to court, I couldn't sleep," he says. "My natural tendency seems to be, 'Why pray when you can worry?'"

Mr. Roberts walked all over the foothills, explaining to God, "This is just too hard, Lord. I can't go through with it."

In answer, God put into his mind a picture of a brick wall. "I was one brick in that wall," Ken Roberts says. "All the other bricks were people who were praying for me and my case. No one of us alone could do much, but by using all of us together, God was building a strong, powerful wall. And it was with this wall that he held back the darkness." Ken Roberts carried that picture of the mighty brick wall with him through two tough years of court battles.

Sometimes the biggest problems show us our need for prayer most clearly. And through those problems we most quickly learn to depend upon God's promises to help us, just as the Old Testament prophet Elijah did.

GOD ANSWERS ELIJAH'S PRAYER

I remembered Elijah's frantic prayers (1 Kings 17 and 18) to God when my husband, Tim, and I were taking a study vacation in the Holy Land. As I stood atop Mount Carmel, looking out at the endless blue sky, I thought of the prophet and the dilemma he faced.

The land of Israel was gripped in a terrible famine. For three years there had not been so much as a tiny drop of dew. "As the Lord God of Israel lives, before whom I stand," Elijah had proclaimed at the beginning of the drought, "there shall not be dew nor rain these years, except at my word." King Ahab, you see, along with his wife Jezebel, had sinned mightily in idol worship. God was exceedingly displeased.

After the country had endured three long years of drought, God told Elijah to go see King Ahab.

"Summon the people from all over Israel to meet on Mount Carmel," Elijah told the king, "and bring the prophets of Baal that are eating at your table with you and Jezebel."

In answer to the challenge, King Ahab gathered together all the prophets of Baal to confront Elijah. All assembled, the count stood at 450 to 1. Seems pretty bad odds for poor Elijah, doesn't it?

Elijah didn't think so. He stood up before the multitude gathered below him and said in a loud voice, "If the Lord is God, follow Him; but if Baal is God, follow him."

The people said nothing.

Elijah continued, "I am the only one of the Lord's prophets left, but Baal had 450 prophets." Then he instructed the people to bring two bulls to the mountain. Baal's prophets would choose one animal and set up on their altar. Elijah would do the same with the other. Then the contest would begin.

"You call on the name of your god," Elijah told Baal's prophets, "and I will call on the name of the Lord. The god who answers by lighting his offering on fire—he is God."

And that's just what they did. Early in the morning, the 450 prophets of Baal began to call on their god. "Oh, Baal, answer us," they pleaded. There was no answer.

By noon, when there was still no answer, Elijah suggested, "Maybe you need to shout louder. Your god could be busy, or perhaps he's traveling. Maybe he's sleeping and needs to be awakened."

So the prophets shouted louder. Still no answer.

Midday passed and evening came. Still no answer.

When night fell, Elijah stepped forward to take his turn. First he dug a deep trench around his altar. Then he instructed the people to fill jars with water and pour it over the altar. They did, soaking both the offering and the wood. Then Elijah told them to do it again. They did. He told them to do it a third time. They did. By then the altar was so soaked that water ran down and filled the trench.

Then Elijah stepped forward and lifted his hands up to God in prayer. "Answer me, Lord," he prayed, "so these people will know you are God, and will turn their hearts back to you."

God answered, all right. The fire He sent from heaven not only burned up the sacrifice, it also consumed the soaked wood, the stones of the altar, and the ground on which the altar stood. It even licked up the water in the trench!

You can imagine how the people reacted. They fell on their faces and cried out, "The Lord—He is God! The Lord—He is God!"

After that victorious showdown, when the crowd had all gone home, Elijah bowed all alone before God on top of Mount Carmel—right where I was standing—and waited for the Lord to send rain. But none came. No rain, no sprinkles, no dew, nothing.

"Go look toward the sea," Elijah said to his

servant who stood a little way off. "See if you can't see a cloud there."

But even toward the sea, where a storm was most likely to develop, all the servant could see in any direction was blue sky. He came back to Elijah and said, "There is nothing."

Again Elijah said, "Go see if there is any cloud."

Again the servant reported back, "There is nothing."

Six times Elijah sent his servant to search the sky. Six times the servant came back with the same reply: "There is nothing."

But Elijah was not about to give up. He sent his servant back yet a seventh time. This time the servant came running back to report, "There is a cloud as small as a man's hand raising out of the sea!"

"That's it!" Elijah exclaimed. "Get ready! There's going to be a deluge of rain!"

Seven times that servant was sent back to check the sky. Here, standing on the mountain, I could see just what the servant saw—nothing but a wide expanse of blue! Yet he kept going back and checking. God made Elijah a promise, and Elijah knew God would keep it.

God has made promises to us too. Here is but a sampling of His promises to those who pray:

Call to Me, and I will answer you, and show you great and mighty things, which you do not know (Jer. 33:3).

Ask, and it will be given to you; seek and you will find; knock, and it will be opened to you. For everyone who asks receives, and he who seeks finds, and to him who knocks it will be opened (Matt. 7:7–8).

If we confess our sins, He is faithful and just to forgive us our sins and to cleanse us from all unrighteousness (1 John 1:9).

Know what God has promised you. Then, when you face trouble or doubt, remember those promises. You can call on God to rescue you just as Elijah did.

God commands us to pray. He has given us promises that depend upon our willingness to pray. And He also shows us how to pray.

A MODEL PRAYER

Our Lord didn't leave us to guess how to pray, nor to hope we are praying as we ought. He gave us a model to follow. We know it as the Lord's Prayer. In *Strength for the Coming Days,* a prayer guide put out by CWA, we find the following six principles that should guide the prayer life of each of us:

"HALLOWED BE YOUR NAME." This first principle is one of praise. This includes both adoration—honoring God for who He is—and thanksgiving—honoring Him for what He has done. What a way to begin our prayers!

"YOUR KINGDOM COME. YOUR WILL BE DONE." This second principle is one of agreeing with God's will and submitting ourselves to it.

"GIVE US THIS DAY OUR DAILY

BREAD." Yes, it is all right for us to ask of God. In fact, Scripture proves that God encourages us to ask for both our own needs and for the needs of others.

"FORGIVE US OUR DEBTS." We are to keep our hearts cleansed by asking the Lord for forgiveness for our sins.

"DELIVER US FROM THE EVIL ONE." Every one of us constantly faces the temptation to sin. We all need God's help to overcome temptation.

"FOR YOURS IS THE KINGDOM AND THE POWER AND THE GLORY FOREVER. AMEN." Isn't this a wonderful ending for our prayers? It elevates the Lord as it brings the prayer to an appropriate close.

What a model! Try using it in your own prayers and watch your prayer life blossom.

We saw a few of Jesus' promises involving prayer. Let's look at one more: "Again I say to you that if two of you agree on earth concerning anything that they ask, it will be done for them by My Father in heaven. For where two or three are gathered together in My name, I am there in the midst of them" (Matt. 18:19–20).

Jesus wants us to pray together. It is His will that we be united in prayer. When we come together before Him, He listens.

UNITED IN PRAYER

Whatever your difficulty, you don't have to go through it alone. When I couldn't pray for myself, my husband prayed for me. Today, people all over the country are praying for me. Many of these "prayer partners" are people I will never meet.

Ken Roberts has people all over the country praying for him too. Our attorneys represented Jolene Cox, of Oxford, Mississippi, in an equal access case. She doesn't know Ken Roberts, but she has heard about his case, and she certainly knows what it's like to go through a trial.

"I have a poster on my wall that reminds me of Ken Roberts in Colorado," Jolene told me. "I hung it on my wall and put a little note on it that says: 'Pray for Ken Roberts.' Every time I pass that poster I think of Ken and say a prayer for him."

I like that. The Scripture tells us to pray for one another. Something visual can be a wonderful way to remind ourselves to pray consistently for someone who needs extra prayer or perhaps someone who may be so down she cannot pray for herself.

Ken had no idea that across the country, in Oxford, Mississippi, a woman he had never met was praying for him many times a day, day after day, week after week, month after month. What he did know was that he had a lot of prayer support. "I didn't have to go through this alone," he says. "I'm all alone in my classroom, and I'm all alone in the school, but people are praying for me. So I'm not really alone after all."

"I really believe it was the prayers of an awful lot of people that kept me from being wiped out a long time ago," Ken Roberts says.

Certainly Ken has every reason to be discouraged and to question our court system. While the judge who heard his case ruled that the Bible, which the principal had ordered removed from the school library, had to be returned, he also ruled that Ken Roberts couldn't read his Bible in class. And Mr. Roberts was told to remove the two Christian books from his classroom library. What the judge seemed to be saying was that if the kids were to see their teacher silently reading the Bible or to see Christian books on his classroom bookshelves, they would think the school endorsed them, and that would be a violation of the Constitution. Yet if they were to see him reading a book on Buddhism or religions of the American Indians, there would be no problem.

"The school district talks about the Bible like it's hazardous waste, like asbestos in the ceiling tiles," Jordan Lorence told the court in his closing arguments. "They make it sound like the Bible can't even be in the same classroom with public school students."

Later the attorney said, "It's a double standard, one that results in everything Christian being filtered out and removed from our public schools."

That doesn't sound much like American religious freedom, does it?

Yes, even in our freedom-loving country there is a great deal to be done. We pledge ourselves to prayer. We must support each other. We must approach God in unity of mind and purpose. And a good place to start is by uniting in prayer right in our own homes.

HUSBAND AND WIFE UNITED IN PRAYER

My husband and I pray together. We started in earnest when our children approached their early teen years. That's when we suddenly realized we *had* to get closer to God. Tim and I had always believed in prayer, and we'd always prayed. But it was at this time that we came upon an idea of how we could pray together in a very special way.

The first night Tim led in prayer about one specific concern he had on his heart. He prayed a brief prayer about it, then I prayed about his concern. Then Tim prayed about his second concern, and I prayed about that concern. He led all the concerns that night, and I followed him on each one, praying specifically for six or seven items on his prayer list.

The second night was my turn to lead. One by one I'd pray for several items on my list of prayer concerns, and each time Tim would follow. The third night was his turn, the fourth night mine.

After about two weeks of praying this way, we could no longer tell Tim's list of concerns from mine. The two had become one.

Isn't this a beautiful way for two hearts united in marriage to be molded together with one mind and one spirit in prayer? It was exciting to be sharing each other's deepest concerns in such an intimate way.

Besides my own prayer time and the prayers I share with my husband, I have a wonderful added bonus—the prayer support of a great many women all around the country. Repeatedly at the end of their letters women say: "I'm praying for you. Please let me know your special prayer requests because I want to know how to pray for you." These women will never know how much they mean to me. Quite simply, I couldn't function without them. I have often told people who receive my CWA mail asking for financial support, that first and foremost is the request for prayer. The monetary support should only follow the prayer commitment.

Prayer is more than important; it is essential. We need to pray and we need to pray faithfully.

THE MECHANICS OF FAITHFUL PRAYER

While in Israel, I went to one of my favorite spots to pray. With my prayer list in hand, I entered the solitude of the Garden Tomb just outside the old wall of the ancient city of Jerusalem. I found a quiet spot under a tree with the tomb close by. The power of the resurrected Christ is why we can come to Him in prayer. We expect Him to have the power to answer just as He promised He would. Some of the things I had on my list seemed a long way from being answered. Some I didn't even know how to pray about properly. But God has promised to hear my prayers. That's His responsibility. Mine is to keep on praying.

It's not enough to simply send up a quick prayer and figure, "Well, there I've done all I can." No, we are to keep going boldly before the Lord with our petitions. That's what Elijah did. And according to Scripture, the sky became black with clouds, the wind came up, and Israel was deluged with rain.

Jesus urged us to be both bold and persistent in our prayers. Right after teaching his disciples the Lord's Prayer, Jesus told them this story:

> Which of you shall have a friend, and go to him at midnight and say to him, "Friend, lend me three loaves; for a friend of mine has come to me on his journey, and I have nothing to set before him;" and he will answer from within and say, "Do not trouble me; the door is now shut, and my children are with me in bed; I cannot rise and give to you"? I say to you, though he will not rise and give to him because he is his friend, yet because of his persistence he will rise and give him as many as he needs (Luke 11:5–8).

Ken Roberts' case is on appeal. He is discouraged. It is my responsibility to pray boldly for him. I have family members who are ill. There are some who need to mend their relationships with the Lord. It is my responsibility to pray persistently for them. My arthritis lurks just below the surface, threatening to keep me from doing what the Lord has for me to do. It is my responsibility to pray faithfully for my health and strength.

Every case in which CWA was involved was on the prayer list I had with me that day at the Garden Tomb. Every staff member was there with his or her special needs noted. Every member of my family was listed. Every state and area leader for CWA was on my list for special prayer. I had a responsibility to pray for each one of them.

Our Nicaraguan refugee work was definitely on my prayer list. A few people just cannot understand why we want to get involved down there. They feel our work with legislation and litigation should be enough. What they don't understand is that what happened in Central America could very well be happening in America within a few years. What's the use of fighting abortion, what's the use of fighting pornography, if we're going to decay from within by the threat of Communism, Marxism and secular humanism?

And furthermore, as Christians we are to care for those who are needy in any way we can. That's what the Scripture teaches. James 5:16 tells us: "The effective, fervent prayer of a righteous man avails much." The suffering Nicaraguan refugees were definitely on my prayer list.

There at the tomb I spent a great deal of time in prayer. But I don't have to be in the Holy Land to pray. I can and do pray daily. It is not only my responsibility to pray consistently, it is my responsibility to pray with loving concern.

I found an old book, that is no longer in print, that contains some of George Washington's prayers written in diary form. On one specific day, in the midst of his prayers, George Washington wrote, "And, Lord, forgive me for my sins. My prayers have become so cold and indifferent that they have become my sin itself." Immediately I was struck by what he was saying.

He's right! Our prayers can become so cold and indifferent they actually become our sin of indifference.

DAILY PRAYER

My day here in Washington starts early. Since I'm at the office by eight-thirty or nine o'clock, my early morning hours at home are critical. I wake up somewhere between five-thirty and six o'clock and pour myself a cup of coffee that my husband has already made for me. Then I turn on the little tape recorder I keep by my bed and listen to tapes of praise music.

I've found I can focus my entire day simply by directing my first thoughts of the morning. The decision is mine: either I can wake up and start worrying about my schedule for the day and the pressures I will face, then move on into a worried hectic day; or I can listen to tapes of praise to God and focus my thoughts above the world. I've determined to start my day praising the Lord.

From there I move into my prayer time. When I start out praising, I can enter my prayer time already in an attitude of worship and adoration and blessing the Lord. With praise songs still playing in the background, I try to have time to slip down on my knees beside my bed and spend time adoring the Lord. Praising and worshiping the Lord is such an important part of prayer, yet it's always a temptation to skip it.

In our busy lives it's too easy to just jump in and give the Lord a shopping list of needs without pausing to worship and praise Him. Yet I've found that when I start off my day with my priorities in order, when I begin with my attention off myself and on the Lord, my attitude for the whole day is different.

From this beginning I can continue to pray all the time I'm getting ready in the morning. I pray while I'm brushing my teeth. I pray while I'm combing my hair. My worship time takes place beside my bed, but I can talk to the Lord about my needs for the day and ask Him for wisdom and share my concerns for myself and for others as I get ready.

By the time I go out the door, I'm uplifted and refreshed. I move my car out onto the highway and into the traffic, I head toward the stacks of work waiting for me on my desk, and I'm excited to face the day. What a contrast to the way I used to live! And I can tell a definite difference when occasionally I skip over my prayer time. I spend the day operating under my own wisdom and strength.

There was a time, before I moved to Washington, when I tried to do everything in my strength. But the pressures I face here have forced me to depend on the Lord and to grow spiritually. Here I *have* to depend on the Lord's help. It is an absolute necessity. I could not do what I'm doing today without the Lord's moment-by-moment help.

I think back to that year when my arthritis was so bad and getting worse every day. I prayed until I could no longer pray, but God was awfully quiet. It is at such times as these, when it takes so much faith and so much perserverance just to keep going, that we need each other so much.

"It would be much easier if God just kept

talking to me all the time, telling me what was going on and what would happen next," Ken Roberts says. "I don't know how it works for other people, but it sure wasn't like that for me. There were an awful lot of quiet times where I just had to draw faith from what He had shown me before."

That's how it is for me too, Ken. And I suspect that's how it is for almost everyone. If we focus on circumstances we get so discouraged at times. During those times it is terribly hard to continue to trust. We want to keep our faith strong, but it wavers in spite of us. These are the times when we have to rely on God's promises to us. At such times it helps to see we're not alone in our discouragement. Yes, Beverly LaHaye has felt that discouragement. And, yes, Ken Roberts has felt it. But we kept on praying and God heard our prayers. "But He hears the prayer of the righteous" (Prov. 15:29).

How should we pray? With worship and praise for God. Persistently and boldly. When we feel like it and when we don't. For ourselves and our needs, and for the needs of others.

Our prayers may not be eloquent. We may stumble and hesitate while we pray. We may grope for words. It doesn't matter, for God knows our hearts.

Colossians 4:2, "Continue earnestly in prayer, being vigilant in it with thanksgiving."

CHAPTER
4

ELEVEN PRINCIPLES OF PRAYER

When I first met Vicki Frost, I didn't know what to expect. I did know she had been arrested for trespassing at her child's school for "an unlawful purpose." And I knew what that purpose was: She was going to take her daughter out of her reading class. The charge was incredible. What kind of a person was this Vicki Frost?

When I met Vicki in Church Hill, Tennessee, I saw a mother who cared about what her eleven-year-old child was reading in her school reading textbook. Mental telepathy. New age thought. Militant feminism. The Frosts were a beautiful example of a good, all-American family who were trying to live by their principles.

"I didn't even try to go to my daughter's classroom," Vicki told me. "I was arrested in the principal's office."

At the time Vicki couldn't believe what was happening to her. "This is America," she said, shaking her head. "What happened to our freedom?"

Like a common criminal, Vicki was carted off to jail.

"It was like I was a character in a play, just sitting back, watching it all happen to someone else," Vicki said. "I couldn't believe it was happening to me!"

In jail Vicki was fingerprinted. Then a metal plaque on a chain was hung around her neck and a mug shot was taken. After being sprayed with an insecticide, she was locked up.

"A prisoner up the hall called out, 'What'd you do?' and I said, 'I wanted to take my child out of her reading class.'"

Because she cared about what her children were being taught, Vicki was a prisoner. There are so many parents in America who could not care less about their kids, whose children are home alone with no one looking after them, and here was a mother who cared—in jail.

To make this humiliating experience worse, Vicki's children were expelled from school and held up for ridicule. The media painted her family and the little group of parents who supported them as fanatics bent on censorship and attacking basic educational materials. For instance, the media stated they were objecting to such works as *The Wizard of Oz* and *Goldilocks and the Three Bears*.

The charge was totally untrue, yet it persisted. Only later did we find how that report got started: People for the American Way had sent a press release to the desks of the editors of all the major newspapers in America stating that Vicki and her supporters were opposed to a long list of classics. The fact that it was totally untrue made no difference at all. Once such misinformation is released and planted in people's minds, it's almost impossible to pull it back.

It was to be five years to the day before the trial would finally end in the halls of the Supreme Court. And during that entire five-year process, the gates of heaven were constantly bombarded by prayer.

LEARNING TO PRAY

Most of us, by God's grace, will never be called upon to go through the ordeal Vicki Frost suffered. Yet every one of us needs to incorporate into our own prayer lives the principles of prayer that characterized those five long years. Let's look at eleven of those principles.

1. *Before you can see an answer to prayer, you must pray.*

"It all started when my eleven-year-old daughter asked me to help her with a question in her reading book," Vicki said. When Vicki read the story, she was amazed to find it had to do with two characters who communicated by means of telepathic thoughts. "It wasn't presented as fiction," Vicki insisted. "It was presented as the wave of the future."

Vicki decided to read on and see what was in the rest of the book. The more she read, the more alarmed she became. In that one reading book, Vicki counted 130 pages that dealt directly or indirectly with mental telepathy. Interwoven with that was evolutionist fact, situational ethics, and a good deal of militant feminism.

"I was utterly astounded at what I was reading!" Vicki told me. "Here I was trying to teach my child the importance of honesty, and her reading book was teaching her it all depended on the circumstances, that sometimes to lie was the best thing to do!"

When Vicki Frost opened that reader, she wasn't looking for a fight. "I didn't even know what secular humanism was," she said. "But the more I read, the more obvious it became that what was in that book was contrary to God's Word."

Worst of all, she began to see a systematic pattern emerging. The teachings that so alarmed her were carefully integrated to make a truly frightening pattern.

"That night I remember going into our bathroom and getting on my knees and praying, 'Dear Lord, how can this be?' I was so overcome by what I had read, I could do nothing but pray."

When we become desperate, when we find ourselves in a situation we absolutely cannot handle alone, we suddenly find the time to pray. Many parents have come to this point when they are dealing with school boards and school curricula.

"When all else fails," Ken Roberts once said ruefully, "we pray."

Yet what God really desires of us is that we go to Him first and foremost. He wants us to pray daily, not just in desperation. It is when we come to Him regularly that we find direction and purpose in our lives.

"You do not have because you do not ask," the apostle James said (James 4:2). These few words give us the reason for the powerlessness the average Christian experiences. We do not live in a praying age. Many, many people today simply do not believe in the power of prayer. But unless we ask, how can God answer? Parents need to ask for wisdom for today's conflicts regarding their children and education.

2. *Prayer is not to be self-centered.*

Vicki Frost truly does believe in prayer. And she believes in Christians supporting one another through prayer. When I visited with Vicki, she took me to the jail where she had been held. As I stood with Vicki in front of that jail and listened to all she had gone through, my heart broke for that poor woman and her family. We prayed together, but her prayer was not for herself. Nor was it for her children and their humiliation nor her husband. Her prayer was for *me*.

How contrary self-centered prayer is to the teaching of Jesus! In the Lord's Prayer, Christ's model for us, we see that words such as *I* and *me* and *mine* are never used. Instead, we read *us* and *our* and *you* and *your*.

Yet, unlike Jesus, we often tend to be extremely self-centered in our praying. Much of what is written and taught about prayer is selfish. We tend to dwell on our own needs and desires and those of our friends and family. That focus is wrong.

Before we pray for ourselves, or even for

others, we are to pray for the glory of God. Of the six requests in the Lord's Prayer, the first three are not for human needs at all. They are for God and His kingdom: "Thy kingdom come, Thy will be done on earth as it is in heaven." The last three are for human needs the world over: "Give us this day our daily bread"; "Forgive us our debts as we forgive our debtors"; "Deliver us from evil."

The concept of prayer that practices a demanding approach to God is arrogant and haughty. Such prayer is destructively simplistic. This presumptuous approach has left a lot of people wounded and bruised. They honestly thought they could come skipping into the throne room of God and get everything on their wish lists. When God didn't respond the way they had been taught He was going to, their faith was shattered.

It is vital that we reach the place where we come into the presence of God acknowledging Him for who He is, not for what He does. This type of prayer draws our focus off ourselves and toward the glory of God. From there we will look to the needs of other people.

This doesn't mean our own personal needs have no place in our prayers. What it does mean is that the closer we come to God, the less selfish our prayers will be.

3. *Successful prayer asks that God's will be done.*

Vicki Frost prayed for her case, you can be sure. Yet she prayed that God's will—whatever it be—be done.

"When we pray, we have to trust God for the outcome," she says. "Whatever it is, He is the one in control. He is sovereign over all affairs. It doesn't matter what it looks like to us."

This isn't an easy philosophy to live by when one is in a predicament such as Vicki's.

"The thing is," Vicki says, "I didn't have the wisdom to know God's purpose. All I knew was that God wanted me to live in truth."

The false arrest case was terribly trying for Vicki. During the close of the oral arguments, the defense was extremely cruel.

"So many lies were being told about me," Vicki says. "They said I was a woman of the world. They said all I wanted was to be a star. They said I was just dragging my husband along on my coattails. I was absolutely crushed!"

When the oral arguments finally ended, Vicki ran to the restroom. Right there on the dirty floor she got down on her knees to pray. "Lord, I'm out on a limb," she prayed. "I have nothing to hang on to but You. I've put You to the test; I'm trying You and I'm proving You." Then she added, "Lord, whatever Your will is, I'm going to hang on to it."

Vicki told me all she could pray was, " 'Lord, Your will be done.' I knew if His will was done, it didn't matter what the outcome was. But I did add, 'Lord *if* it can be Your will for me to win, I sure would appreciate it!' "

As it worked out, it *was* His will that Vicki won in having the criminal charges against her dismissed, even though she lost the appeal to have her children opt out of class. "I have appreciated the victories so much," Vicki says, "and I have learned to accept the losses as God's will for us."

Without a doubt the most effective prayer is the prayer that is according to the will of God.

4. *When you pray, pray strenuously.*

From a formerly quiet life as a self-described mother and housewife who spent her days cooking and cleaning and caring for her family, Vicki suddenly found herself unwittingly thrust into media headlines. She was now the focus of two radically different opinions. "Some people supported me, but others wrote letters to the editor against me."

It wasn't only the media, either. People for the American Way organized rallies. "In one they gathered one thousand people together, then encouraged the crowd to march against us like an army," Vicki reports.

And things got worse. The juvenile judge threatened to jail the Frost children if they didn't go back into their classrooms. The principal had written a letter to the district attorney asking the state to "intervene in order to bring some reality into the Frost situation." Finally, the Frosts took their children out of the public school system and enrolled them in a private Christian school.

The worse things became, the more earnestly Vicki Frost and her family prayed.

James 5:17 talks about praying earnestly. Luke 22:44 talks about *more* earnestly praying. After reading these two portions of Scripture one day, I started wondering: Just what does "more earnestly praying" mean? Earnestly, I can understand. But more earnestly?

According to the Greek, earnestly implies praying with fervor. Well, if that's earnestly, how in the world does one pray more earnestly? I looked up the Greek definition on that verse, and here is what it said: "To be stretched out or to strenuously pray." Another synonym is "exhaustively praying."

Strenuously pray! How peculiar! When I think of something strenuous, I think of exercising or of doing hard physical work. I think of sweating and straining, panting and aching. How could anyone pray so hard that sweat would literally pour off one's face?

Then I remembered Jesus. He prayed until He sweat drops of blood! And Rachel in the book of Jeremiah cried uncontrollably for her children and would not be comforted.

What would it take for us as Christians to exercise the kind of prayer that causes us to be stretched out before God? If we are to pray as Jesus did, we need to learn more about exhausting ourselves when we pray.

5. *God answers specific prayers.*

"During the preliminary hearing, we'd had a *terrible* day in court," Vicki recalled. "The judge was really hostile toward us. There was an ice storm going on outside, and our witnesses were late. The judge said, 'If they can't get here, that's your problem. I'm here, and if they aren't, that's just too bad'."

It was an exasperating situation. Vicki and

our CWA attorneys left the courtroom and went to the hotel room and prayed, "Lord, please stop this trial. Please give us some time. Our witnesses have not been allowed to testify. We've been cut off."

The next day they got a phone call. Court was canceled. The night before, as Vicki and the attorneys were praying, two jury members had been injured on the way home. The judge himself had to have emergency surgery. All three were in the hospital.

"That's not what we prayed for," Vicki insists. "We just prayed for help."

They prayed specifically—that God would stop the trial, that they would be given some time. Court didn't resume for four months. God heard their prayer.

In Ephesians 6:18 we are instructed to pray "always with all prayer and supplication." Then we are told to be watchful—or as another translation says, to be alert. In other words, we are to be informed. And then we are to speak boldly.

While it is appropriate to ask God to open up our narrow, limited view, sometimes it is up to us to become informed so that we can pray as we ought. We need to educate ourselves about the particular situation, so that our prayers won't be limited to generalities.

God answered a specific prayer for me and thousands of others when Madalyn Murray O'Hair filed a lawsuit against CWA, Beverly LaHaye, and some other organizations. She had charged us with a libel suit when we exposed her growing anxiety to have "In God we trust" removed from our currency and coins.

It could have been a critical court decision

by a jury. So many hours were spent in preparing for our day in court. We could not understand why the judge was so long to respond to our numerous requests to have the case dismissed. We felt from the beginning that it was a "frivolous" case, and we asked thousands of churches and CWA members to pray specifically. Our prayers were to have the case dismissed.

Ten days before we were to appear in court to begin the case, we received the call that the judge had dismissed every charge against us. God had answered the specific prayers of so many!

If we are to pray with power, we must set aside vague prayers. Those prayers may be beautiful; they may be charmingly phrased. But if they ask no definite specific thing, we can expect no definite, specific answer.

6. *God will give you specific direction if you ask for it.*

Often women ask me, "Beverly, how do you get your direction on what to do?" What I do is begin jotting down a line or two to pray about. As earnestly as I can, I start praying about that subject. Many times an amazing thing happens. In the middle of my prayer time, the whole thing opens up, and I begin to see a new way to proceed. Sometimes it's an entirely different approach on what to do, how to do it, how much to do, or where to do it.

Let me give you an example. A few years ago it became obvious that we were growing to a place where we needed some sort of a communications department. In our early days, the media usually ignored us, and we were the best kept secret in America. But as we began to do more lobbying and our field development began to grow and our litigation in the courts expanded and became better known, it became more and more clear that we had to have some sort of department devoted to communications. To gain credibility, it was time to let the public know about our involvements and successes.

The problem is, I had never worked in this area before. So on my prayer list the best I could do was put "Public Relations." I couldn't be any more specific because I just didn't know enough about what was involved or what to ask for. As I prayed, I asked the Lord, "Do we need a public relations department? Should we hire a PR person, or can we just do what needs to be done on our own?"

Right there in my bedroom, as I prayed over these questions, I began to be enlightened on various aspects. The answers came: "Well, of course, you need a communications department, Beverly, because you need to be training grassroots leaders in each state and each community. They need to know how to deal with issues too. It's not just your need here in Washington. Ladies in Iowa need to know how to communicate to the media. Ladies in Arizona need to know how to do a press conference."

Until then I had been focusing only on our communications needs here in Washington, D.C. Now I suddenly began to get a broader picture of what we should be doing and where the Lord was leading us.

This was from the Lord. It had to be because I wasn't experienced enough in these matters to think of any of this on my own.

Today we have a communications department. What's more, we have a communications coordinator in every state where we have an area representative; that person is responsible for training women in all areas of media communication. These coordinators are taught to face the media, instructed in how to hold a press conference, shown how to write a press release, and informed on many other valuable techniques. And it all started with that simple little phrase on my prayer list.

How is your picture of the issues you face in your own life? Perhaps, as mine was, it is extremely narrow. Start praying, and trust the Lord to open up that picture. We often put limits on God in our personal life simply because we make decisions based on our own limitations instead of on God's greatness.

7. *Prayer must be accompanied by action.*

From the beginning, the motto of Concerned Women for America has been "Protecting the rights of the family through prayer and action"—in that order.

Vicki Frost insists that before her involvement in the textbook case, she would never have considered herself a politically active person. The mother of four young children, she was totally involved in her home and in raising her family. "I love to sew and cook and clean," she says. "Since the time I was married, I've been busily occupied as a housewife." She didn't even belong to the PTA. "I might go once a year to something at school, but I certainly didn't go down to check on my children, or their teachers, or anything like that. I was busy taking care of my home."

And now? "I would never want to be that way again!" Vicki says.

What an example! Concern produces prayer, prayer produces action, and action brings results. Prayer must come first, then action naturally follows. It is when we come from the prayer closet that our actions truly demonstrate the character and spirit and nature of Christ. We are only as effective in the world as we are effective in our prayer life.

I really don't believe it is possible to be an effective prayer and not also be an activist. For when we have been in the presence of God, we are going to come out doing something. What we do will vary with our own individual calling and gifts, but whatever our action is, we are going to get involved. Prayer isn't hiding from problems; it's getting our marching orders.

Often people who have received their marching orders directly from God join with us without our even asking them. Vicki Frost found this to be true in her case.

Vicki was on her way to her preliminary hearing. The purpose of the hearing was for the prosecution to bind her over for trial on the charge of trespassing. If she were found guilty, her sentence would quite possibly be two years in jail.

As she entered the foyer with her husband

and a group of friends, she came face-to-face with an older lady standing by the door. The woman looked at the group surrounding Vicki and asked, "What are you here for?"

Vicki told her about the hearing and the charge against her.

"Well," the lady said, "now I know why *I'm* here."

The woman explained that she regularly ministered to the female inmates in the lower jail. "Today I felt the Holy Spirit was telling me to come and stand here and wait for Him to let me know what to do. Now I know. I'm supposed to pray for you."

Now Vicki had never seen this woman before, and the lady knew absolutely nothing about the case. But they went together to a back room, away from the courtroom traffic, and the woman began to pray.

"She prayed Scripture," Vicki told me. "Scripture and Scripture and more Scripture came from her mouth."

One verse in particular stuck in Vicki's mind: "The LORD will fight for you, and you shall hold your peace" (Ex. 14:14).

From the calming encouragement of that impromptu prayer meeting, Vicki Frost went into the extremely tense environment of the preliminary hearing, "an ordinary housewife and mother from the mountains of Tennessee," Vicki says, "all of a sudden in the courtroom and accused of a crime."

The school system was well represented that day. School board members were there along with principals and many, many teachers. The courtroom was packed. Onlookers stood three and four deep in the back. Not another person could have been squeezed into that room. "All those people were there to see me bound over to a grand jury," Vicki says.

And the crowd was hostile. Some of the school personnel actually kicked the people who had come to support Vicki!

For Vicki that first preliminary hearing, charging her with trespassing on the school grounds, was a tough, exasperating experience. The testimony of the testifying officer, who happened to be the Church Hill chief of police, was basically a fabrication. The more she heard, the harder it was for Vicki to keep quiet. "I so badly wanted to say, 'That's just not true!' I wanted to say *something* to defend myself, but I never had the opportunity."

"You shall hold your peace," she recalled the Scripture the woman had prayed with Vicki that morning. "The Lord will fight for you." Now Vicki was beginning to understand. God was going to deliver her, and she was not going to have a thing to do with it.

At the end of the preliminary hearing the judge twice cautioned the courtroom, "If anyone makes an outburst of any kind, I'll find you in contempt of court." It was a tense situation. Then he read his decision: There was no probable cause for the arrest and no Tennessee statute that would back up the charge. Case dismissed.

As Vicki left the courtroom that day, several reporters ran up. All she could say was the Scripture the lady had prayed: "You shall hold your peace. The Lord will fight for you."

"The Lord *did* fight for me, and He won!" Vicki announced triumphantly. The next morning the headlines in *The Kingsport Daily News* read: "Lord Wins Trespass Case."

The Lord heard Vicki Frost's prayers.

8. *God delights in Scripture.*

The unknown woman who prayed for Vicki before her preliminary hearing obviously practiced the principle of praying Scripture. I too have found that a most rewarding way to pray. So much so that at CWA's Tenth Anniversary Celebration I gave each of our attending members a copy of *Strength for the Coming Days*, a book I frequently use as part of my own prayer time. As I said in the foreword of this book, praying scripturally will help us to stand firm in these evil days.

Strength for the Coming Days is divided into three major parts. First is a topical arrangement of Scripture prayers (prayers for personal needs, for instance, or for forgiveness or renewal). If Vicki had looked under this section during her trial, she would have found several scriptural prayers to pray, such as, "LORD , it is nothing for You to help, whether with many or with those who have no power; help us, O LORD our God, for we rest on You, and in Your name we go against this multitude. O LORD, You are our God; do not let man prevail against You!" which is quoted from 2 Chronicles 14:11.

The second section of this book presents

four suggested approaches to yearly Bible reading and memorization. I find that when I have to face persons who are openly antagonistic, as Vicki did, Scripture can help me present a calm exterior—and more important, an inner calmness as well. Vicki Frost was praying for God's will, and Scripture prayers for God's will to be done are found in that special area of the memory verses.

The final section is the one that is most useful to me: a day-by-day pattern of scriptural prayers for thirty-one days (one each day for adoration, forgiveness, renewal, personal needs, intercession, affirmation, and thanksgiving). As I go through this daily plan, I am unconsciously memorizing Scripture at the same time that I am praying God's Word back to Him. What a rewarding way to talk to my Lord!

9. *More things are wrought by prayer than this world dreams of.*

"The effective, fervent prayer of a righteous man avails much" (James 5:16). These words of God set forth prayer as a force that brings things to pass that would not be were it not for prayer. God has chosen to limit His action in response to the prayers of His people. That's the way He works.

It isn't needs that God responds to. He responds to prayer. If God responded to need, there wouldn't be any. We often look at a problem and say, "Why doesn't God *do* something about it?" It just may be that He is waiting for us to become involved—to pray, then to act.

Let me tell you about the prayer of Jim

Woodall, our CWA director of Latin American affairs in charge of our refugee projects. As a missionary in Central America, Jim realized the enormity of the problem there. However hard he worked, he was making little impact. The needs were just too great for one person alone.

Jim began to pray specifically that God would send him people who would be concerned for the well-being of the Nicaraguan refugees. And while he prayed, he acted. Leaving his family in Costa Rica, he came back to the States to try to raise interest and funds for helping the refugees. Immediately people started giving him my name.

It was no secret that I, too, was concerned about the plight of the Nicaraguan refugees. For two years I had knocked on doors and made endless telephone calls, trying to find some organization that would let us assist down there. All I found were closed doors. Discouraged, I finally resigned myself to the fact that if God wanted me to do something, He was going to have to make it happen.

I kept praying. God did begin to make it happen in a most miraculous way. After going on a fact-finding trip to visit a refugee camp in Costa Rica, we put together a project we called "Love, Hope, and Apples." This project was organized by a missionary, Michael Lynch, whom I had met several years before in South America. We sent out a brochure to our mailing list and started collecting money for a one-time distribution for a refugee camp in Costa Rica. Sixteen of our CWA leaders were planning to accompany me on this work trip.

Out in California, during this time, Jim

Woodall was given one of our brochures. He could tell immediately that we didn't understand the refugee problem. He tried to call but was never able to reach me. After several attempts, he gave up. All he could do, he decided, was to keep praying that God would make a connection.

It was in January 1987 at the National Religious Broadcasters convention in Washington, D.C., that Jim and I finally met—briefly and by "chance." We talked about Nicaraguan refugees in Costa Rica. He had suggestions and offered his help, but my program was all planned. After about ten minutes we exchanged business cards and parted.

Late that night I received a telephone call telling me that Michael Lynch's sixteen-year-old daughter had just been in a head-on automobile collision and was in a coma. Michael, who had planned to oversee our trip to Costa Rica, now would most likely be unable to go. This was just two weeks before our scheduled trip, and humanly speaking it seemed the only answer was to cancel the trip.

Several of us prayed, "Lord, if we're not supposed to go, this is certainly Your chance to say, 'Forget it,'" But the Lord had other plans.

That's when Jim Woodall came to my mind. I had just met him that very day, and he had offered to help, but at the time everything seemed to be under control. An emergency meeting was arranged for the next day, and I asked him very contritely, "Would you help us?" He replied, of course, that he would.

He did, and God blessed abundantly. It later

became evident that we definitely needed Jim Woodall—not only on that first trip but also in God's future plans for CWA and the refugees in the years ahead. Today the refugee work is a regular part of CWA's program, and Jim is a full-time staff member. It all came about because of prayer and the willingness to wait on the Lord.

10. *Pray over and over again.*

The judge who first heard Vicki Frost's textbook case in 1983 ruled against her and immediately dismissed it. When the case was retried before him in 1986, God had completely changed the man's heart. The second time, the judge ruled in our favor. The difference? Prayer. We prayed for the judge; we prayed for wisdom; we prayed for guidance. God heard our prayers and brought His power to our case.

We didn't simply pray and leave it, either. We kept on praying. Our CWA prayer chapters prayed. Our attorneys and other staff prayed. Vicki prayed. I prayed. I believe women ought to pray and pray and pray some more. There's power in repetitive prayer.

As a child I was taught to tell God what was on my mind one time, then to leave it with him. I was told we never needed to repeat our prayers. Faith meant leaving my concerns with God. Well, that's not what I read in the Bible. We are to go back to our Lord again and again. He wants to hear from us. When we keep on praying, we are demonstrating our expectation of an answer.

In Luke 18:2–5, Jesus tells His disciples a

parable to demonstrate to them the importance of praying and never giving up:

> There was in a certain city a judge who did not fear God nor regard man. Now there was a widow in that city; and she came to him, saying, "Avenge me of my adversary." And he would not for a while; but afterward he said within himself, "Though I do not fear God nor regard man, yet because this widow troubles me, I will avenge her, lest by her continual coming she weary me."

If we are serious about our prayers, we will bring them to the Lord again and again. That's the way He has instructed us to pray.

The first time I went to Costa Rica with Jim Woodall, he told me about his dream—to build a school for the Nicaraguan refugee children. Many of these children had never had the opportunity to go to school, and others had gone briefly but were taught by Cuban Marxist teachers, so their parents kept them out of school.

Now, children and their education are very close to my heart. I wanted to know more about what Jim had in mind.

A few weeks later Jim chartered a plane, and we flew into a small jungle airport in Costa Rica. After a two-hour boat trip up a jungle river, Jim showed me his jungle property. Because of so much thick underbrush it was not terribly impressive.

"Here's where I would like to build a school," he told me as he pointed out into the wild jungle.

Everyone said the school was impossible, but Jim refused to give up. He prayed about it and he prayed about it and he prayed about it some more. People repeatedly told him, "Jim, it won't happen. It's crazy. It's impossible. That place is just too remote." But this was where the people were living, so this was where Jim felt God wanted him to build the school.

I looked around at the thick jungle. And, sure enough, I could see it! I could see the school that was to be.

And so I began to pray along with Jim. As I prayed, I knew I had to take a step of faith and *do* something. I came back to the United States and began to share what I'd seen and learned. I brought back pictures and showed the faces of the little children who would be going to that jungle school. We gradually began to gain support in both money and workers.

From the first church at which I spoke came a team of sixteen men who said, "We'd like to go there this summer and help build that school!"

Those men were the pioneers. They cut through the thick jungle, leveled the ground, and started pouring the foundation. They lived right there in the jungle in little pup tents—some of them had never before been out of the city—and the conditions were terrible! What they encountered was the hottest, most humid jungle weather imaginable. The mosquitoes were huge. Snakes and monkeys lurked in the trees and on the ground. Yet the men worked from sunrise to sunset. When the sun went down, they had to go to bed because if they dared light so much as one little candle, all the bugs in the jungle came to it.

Yet, by faith, those men wanted to do something that would be an answer to prayer. And what God did within those sixteen men is itself a miracle. They went back home transformed. Wives sent us letters saying, "Thank you for sending me a new husband."

And you know what? Today there is a school on that jungle property providing a Christian education to Nicaraguan children. Every morning the school boat heads up the river to pick up the children and bring them to school. A school in the jungle for almost one hundred refugee children! And it came about because Jim refused to give up. He saw the need, he knew God could meet it, and he prayed.

A judge's changed heart . . . a school in the jungle . . . what power persistent, repetitive prayers can bring into our lives!

11. *Not everyone's prayers are answered.*

Many people believe that all the promises in God's Word concerning prayer are made to everyone, and that anyone can claim them. Not so. These promises are made to His children who keep His commandments, who do the things that are pleasing in His sight.

Proverbs 15:8 tells us that "the prayer of the upright is His delight."

Remember James 5:16: "The effective, fervent prayer of a *righteous* man avails much" (emphasis added). A righteous person is one who has a right relationship with God that comes from submission and obedience. Righteousness is not goodness. Nor is it a matter of earning a place with God. It is a position we have been given. Those of us who have accepted Christ as Savior are part of His family. Only if one knows God personally can he have a right to expect God to hear and answer his prayers.

What is your relationship with God? Are you just casually acquainted? Or are you and God intimate friends?

Another hindrance to answered prayer is wrong motives. What should our motive be? According to 1 Corinthians 10:31, "Whatever you do, do all to the glory of God." Our prayers then should have the end result of glorifying God.

CHAPTER
5

FIVE LEVELS OF COMMUNICATION WITH GOD

"Lord, teach us to pray," Jesus' disciples asked of their master.

Considering all the things they could have asked, what an incredible request this was. But there was something about the way Jesus talked with His Father, something about the intimacy that made the disciples long to learn the secret of prayer as He practiced it.

The disciples' understanding of a relationship with God was based on a national concept. They wanted a king who would cast off the shackles of Rome and make Israel a country to be reckoned with. What Jesus portrayed was a personal, one-to-one relationship with God. There was a level of intimacy between Him and His Father the disciples couldn't begin to comprehend.

Learning to know God—really to *know* Him—transformed the disciples' prayer life. It will do the same for us. But this can only be accomplished by moving into deeper levels of communication with God through increasingly personal, intimate prayer. And once our prayer lives are transformed, every niche and every recess of our beings will be revolutionized.

Ever since she was a young child, Evelyn Smith has been a Christian. She knows God's Word, and she is determined to live by it.

During their thirty years of marriage, Mrs. Smith and her husband purchased four one bedroom apartments in Chico, California. Now that she is a widow, the rent she collects from these apartments makes up a significant portion of her income.

When a couple called in response to her rental advertisement, she told them her policy was to rent only to nonsmokers, people who didn't have pets, and, if the applicants were a couple, to those who were married. It is important to her that she not have couples in her houses who are just living together.

"Fornication is a sin," she says, "I don't want any part of it."

The applicants assured Mrs. Smith they were indeed married. But when they came to sign the lease, they admitted that they had lied to her. They weren't really married at all. Mrs. Smith responded by telling them, "Thank you for your honesty." Then she returned their deposit.

A few months later, Mrs. Smith was contacted by officials from the California Department of Fair Employment and Housing. They were investigating a charge that she had engaged in illegal marital status discrimination. In the end the department filed legal charges against her.

"I couldn't understand it," Mrs. Smith says. "To me, it's entirely a moral issue. I mean, if I had a commercial building, there's no way in the world I would rent it out for a sinful purpose—prostitution or an abortion clinic or a pornographic bookstore or anything like that. This was the same thing."

So strong are Evelyn Smith's biblical beliefs and convictions that she determined she would leave the apartments empty rather than rent them to unmarried couples. "If I allowed them to live together on my property, I would be condoning their actions," she insists, "and that is something I cannot do!"

What made the charge even more incomprehensible is the fact that California has accepted for itself the very moral code Mrs. Smith is attempting to uphold. All nineteen California state college campuses forbid unwed couples to live together on campus.

"Why is it lawful for an unwed couple to lease her duplex, but unlawful for the same couple to share a room at the state university two miles away?" asks columnist James J. Kilpatrick. "Why must she be compelled to condone the very kind of immorality the state condemns?"

Unable to find an attorney she could afford who would take her case, Evelyn Smith was beside herself. "I came to the point where I was going to handle the case on my own," she admits. "I didn't want to, but I didn't know what else to do. I prayed, 'Lord, if You want me to do this myself I will, but You sure are going to have to help me.'"

God answered Mrs. Smith's prayer by bringing her to the attention of Concerned Women for America. We agreed to take her case.

When her case was heard, the administrative law judge issued a ruling finding Mrs. Smith guilty of marital status discrimination. He fined her $454 and ordered her to post two signs in each of her rental units, one stating the state law on housing discrimination and the other giving details on how she had lost her case. "He wanted prospective tenants to see that she had been convicted as a bigot," Attorney Lorence claimed.

Mrs. Smith appealed the ruling to the California Commission on Unfair Employment and Housing. Not only did they agree with the lower judge, they upped the fine to $954 and insisted she sign her name to the posted signs!

Often when I challenge women to pray about an issue—sometimes personal, sometimes a matter of national concern for families—the answer will be: "But I *have* prayed! Every day I ask for God's blessings," or "I asked God to stop the legal slaughter of unborn babies in this country," or "I begged God to prevent our legislature from making this decision, but they did it anyway."

But as we saw in Chapter 4, all prayer is not alike. Have you ever noticed how some people come out of a prayer time refreshed and blessed and bubbling over with answers they have received while others look upon prayer as a chore that accomplished little?

What about your own prayer time? Are you one who sees results? If not, you can be!

Prayer, you see, is progressive. Each stage is more personal than the one before. Each brings us greater intimacy with our Father.

Let me share with you what I call the five levels of communications with God:

LEVEL ONE: PRAYER CLICHÉS

"Bless our home."

"Bless us all."

"Thank you for this food."

"God bless America."

"Be with the missionaries all over the world."

Clichés are expressions that have been so overused they no longer mean much. It's the same with prayer clichés. They are those cute little statements the majority of Christians use in their prayers, but they have little meaning. Sad to say, most Christians never move beyond these memorized statements.

I can remember the days before CWA when my prayers for our country were not more than, "God bless America. God bless the president."

Prayer clichés aren't specific. They don't show real concern. Nor do they demonstrate a true understanding of what is at stake. Instead of saying, "God bless America," ask yourself, what exactly is it you want God to do for our country. Rid our land of abortion? Then pray about that issue specifically. Are there particular legislators or bills you need to support? Pray for them by name. Are you concerned about our religious freedoms? Pray specifically for and mark cases such as the one in which Evelyn Smith is involved.

Had Mrs. Smith looked at her problem and then prayed a cliché prayer, she might have said something like this: "Lord, help me. Make everything work out all right." Now, there is nothing wrong with asking for God's help, but what exactly did Mrs. Smith want from God? Wisdom? That He would use her as a witness to His faithfulness? That He would send her people who could advise her and guide her through the trial?

If you are praying, "God bless our home" why not pray more specifically and tell the Father precisely what you want Him to do. It opens up the secret places of your heart to the Lord.

On such a superficial, impersonal level, prayers are largely ineffectual. If this is where you are, it's time you moved on to a higher level.

LEVEL TWO: IMPERSONAL INFORMATION

A great deal of prayer is nothing more than describing a problem to God. It is simply giving the Lord information, bringing Him up to date on our needs. In short, it is a feeble attempt to instruct Him, as though He had no other way of knowing what is happening in our lives!

An example of impersonal praying would be telling God: "Lord, our country is in trouble. There's crime, drugs, corruption. If something isn't done, our children won't have a chance." That may all be true, but it's nothing the Lord doesn't already know.

We need to go beyond telling God the problem. We might say: "Lord, our country cannot get out of its problems unless we as a nation turn to You. I pray that You will open the hearts of ministers to preach against sin from the pulpit. I pray that You will work in the hearts of mothers and fathers to strengthen the home and to teach children right and wrong."

Had Evelyn Smith settled for informational prayer, she would likely have told God: "Lord, I have a problem. I'm being taken to court because I tried to follow your moral standards. I was sure I was doing the right thing, and now this has happened. Now I don't know what to do."

When we pray, we need to go beyond simply telling God *about* our problems. Prayers filled with information are horizontal prayers between two human beings, not between a mortal and an omnipotent God. What we want to do is pray vertically—upward to the Almighty God whose strength and power are far greater than ours.

In the early days of CWA, when we had no idea what we were getting into or where we were going, it was easy to fall into the information type of praying. We couldn't even guess what God was going to do for us. Then came the White House Conference on Families. We wanted to do something, but we just didn't know what we could do. We kept hearing how the White House was selecting delegates who were liberal and wanted to see such things as homosexual marriages sanctioned and given the rights and benefits of a family.

I'm afraid some of our praying came close

to whining: "Here's this government-sponsored organization coming along talking about families and trying to change the definition of a family. Lord, You're the one who instituted the family unit. We are losing our stand for what is right." We wanted to pray specifically, but we just didn't know what to pray for.

When we are frustrated, when we have no idea what to do about a situation, it's easy for us to find ourselves caught in this second level of prayer. It's hard to pray specifically when we are so confused and uncertain.

Since CWA was first founded in 1979, I have tried to start every morning asking God to give me just the amount of wisdom I would need for that day. Now, God knows I lack wisdom in certain areas. And He knows I am badly in need of discretion and discernment. He doesn't need me to tell Him. But by opening my soul to the Lord, by acknowledging my weaknesses specifically and stating exactly what it is I am asking God to do for me that day, I am able to pray more beyond impersonal information and into personal communication.

God knows our needs. He knows our specific situations and the exact difficulties each of us faces. He knows the burdens and desires of our hearts. Of course we should discuss these things with Him, but we need to move beyond a mere recitation of information. We need to talk specifically and personally about what we desire God to do for us right now, in the particular situation we are facing this day and this moment.

God knew the facts of Evelyn Smith's case.

And He knew what was at stake. She didn't need to tell Him that. What she did pray was, "Lord, I want to be an example to those around me. Help me to stand up for God's laws in such a way that others will be encouraged to live by their own convictions."

LEVEL THREE: GIVING YOUR OPINIONS AND CONCLUSIONS TO GOD

Most prayer and a great deal of preaching on the subject of prayer are based on "my need," "my want," and "my desire." More people spend the majority—if not all—of their prayer time telling God what He needs to do about a certain issue or problem and when He needs to do it. How incredibly presumptuous!

After reading a newspaper article about Evelyn Smith and how her Christian convictions led her to take a stand that resulted in the suit being filed against her, a Christian lady from New Jersey telephoned her. After they talked for a while, the subject of prayer came up. The lady confided, "I'm forty-four years old, and I've never been married. I really would love to have a husband. Is it wrong to pray for something like this?"

"There's nothing you shouldn't pray about," Evelyn Smith told the lady.

How true! We can come to our Lord about anything that concerns us. But we need to be careful that we don't end up telling Him what He should do about that concern. Yes, the lady in New Jersey should discuss her fears and her longings with the Lord. She should tell Him she would love to have a husband but after she has shared the desires of her heart with the Lord she needs to wait for the Lord's will and timing. We are not to tell the Lord what His will is for us.

When we come to the Lord in faith, we come willing to trust in His wisdom and His timing. It may be that God will see fit to give the lady a husband. It may be that she will one day have the children she longs for. Or it may be that God will have some other answer for her that she can't yet see. When we pray in faith, we admit to God that we don't have the answers. It is enough to know He will provide the right answers in the right way and the right time.

LEVEL FOUR: SHARE YOUR FEARS AND DREAMS AND GOALS WITH GOD

Because of the media coverage of her case, Evelyn Smith has been asked to appear on a number of talk shows. "But I feel so inadequate!" she told me. "Now if I was like you, if I could speak eloquently . . ."

I had to laugh inside. *If only she knew!* I thought. I was no natural-born spokesperson. My whole life I had been shy and fearful and terribly self-conscious. But when God had a job for me to do, He gave me the ability to do it. I knew He would do the same for Mrs. Smith if she shared her fear with Him.

"If only I could go on television and tell people it really *does* help to be a Christian," Mrs. Smith said to me. "If I could just let them know we truly *do* get comfort from the Lord. I would tell them not to draw conclusions from what has happened in my case so far. I would say, 'Just wait! God hasn't finished yet.'"

Yes, Evelyn Smith does have fears. But what a dream she has! What a goal! It's these dreams and goals, as well as her fears, that she needs to share in detail with the Lord.

Actually, Evelyn Smith does make it a habit to pray specifically and personally. She regularly approaches her time with God by first acknowledging who and what He is—all wise, all knowing, all loving.

The worst result of sin was the separation of the intimacy that was meant to exist between God and man. When we reach this fourth level of communication with God, we are moving back into a position of real intimacy with our Lord. Here we move away from talking with God merely in a corporate, religious way and begin to walk with Him in an intimate, personal way. For when you begin to share your dreams, your goals, your fears, and your emotional distresses with the Lord, you cannot help but be personal.

In addition to her already personal prayer, Evelyn Smith might want to lay before the Lord the very thoughts she shared with me. She might pray, "Lord, I would love to be able to go on television and tell people it really *does* help to be a Christian. I long to let them know I truly *do* get comfort from You. I so want to tell them to wait and watch and see what You are going to do for me. Yet, more than anything, I want You to use me as You see fit. If it could be before a great audience, then, Lord, please give me the opportunity and the ability. If not, then use me just where I am."

LEVEL FIVE: PRAYING INTIMATELY
FOR OTHERS

A trial is a wearying ordeal. With appeals, a case can drag out for years. Add to this the criticisms, negative publicity, and invasions of privacy that often come, and it isn't hard to understand why many people decide it just isn't worth it. But not Evelyn Smith. She is determined to see this case through.

"I have no choice," she says. "I can't give in and I can't give up."

Neither can she do it alone.

"I have a lot of friends who have been praying for me all along," Mrs. Smith says. "I don't know what I would do without them. But what gives me so much extra strength is all the many people I don't even know who write and tell me they are praying for me. Imagine! These are people who don't even know me, yet they take the time to write and say they care."

When you know Christ at such a level that you consistently come before Him in adoration, when with a truly contrite heart you open your soul before Him, then you can become involved in intercessory prayer. Here, at this fifth level of communication with God, you are finally stretched out in prayer. Here your time with the Lord becomes truly strenuous. What a far cry from the early levels of parroting simplistic prayer clichés!

I firmly believe that intercessors are dear to the heart of God. Those who pray personally, intimately, and selflessly on the behalf of others are very special people.

As Paul says in Colossians 4:12, "Epaphras, who is one of you, a servant of Christ, greets you, always laboring fervently for you in prayers, that you may stand perfect and complete in all the will of God."

I thank God for people who "labor fervently" for me in prayer that I might stand perfect and complete in the will of God. This is intercessory prayer.

We all can pray for others. Not only is it our privilege, it is our responsibility.

When I was in Israel praying at the Garden Tomb, I prayed for my grandson who was born with a hearing deficiency, a chest that didn't fully develop, and jaw bones that failed to grow properly. He has been through so much! Now twelve years old, the boy has had to endure four surgeries and faces still more.

During my grandson's last surgery, the doctors took three ribs to extend his jaw and create two joints. During the operation, the intravenous needle feeding saline solution into his arm slipped, and the fluid infiltrated his arm rather than into his vein. Because a surgical drape was covering the boy's arm, a good deal of time went by before anyone realized what was happening. By the time the doctor moved enough for the anesthesiologist to see the problem, the little guy's arm had turned blue up to his elbow and was swollen beyond recognition.

Immediately the doctors stopped the surgery and turned their attention to his arm. They had to open his arm from the palm of his hand to above the elbow to release the pressure and fluid. The situation was so severe that for a while it looked as though it would be necessary to amputate his arm.

"Oh God," I prayed through my tears, "hasn't this dear child suffered enough? God, I know you know best, and most of all I pray for Your will and purpose to be accomplished, but if it be possible, please save my grandson's arm. Give the doctors wisdom and discernment as they deal with this emergency. And, Lord, please lay Your hand on this child I love so much. Engulf him in Your love."

My grandson didn't lose his arm. In fact, despite the terrible scar that runs from his wrist to just above his elbow, he has come out beautifully. He now has a jaw! All things considered, his face looks wonderful.

Months later, on my knees before the Lord at the Garden Tomb, I thanked God all over again for all He'd done for my grandson. Then I prayed for His continued work in the life of this young man—so bright, so gifted in so many ways, but with such a great deal still to overcome. I thanked God for him and for how much he means to us. I prayed for strength and courage for him. Most of all, remembering his cry, "Why me? Why did all this have to happen to me?"—I prayed that he would be able to accept himself just as he is.

I am firmly convinced my grandson has a great and wonderful contribution to make in this life, and I am committed to praying him over the hurdles that lie before him. I will do for him what my husband did for me when I was in such need. That day at the tomb I was overwhelmed by a reassurance from the Lord that everything was going to be all right for that dear boy.

What a privilege to pray on someone else's behalf! How indescribably exciting to watch the answers unfold! Every one of us should be involved in intercessory prayer.

Time spent praying on level five is time of incredible closeness, time when I feel I can almost reach out and touch my Lord. It's so special, so intimate, that I wonder how I ever allow myself to be satisfied with a lesser level. And yet I do. I find myself relating the specifics of legal cases such as Evelyn Smith's to the Lord. Then I find myself telling Him just how He should work out the details. Even though I know without a doubt that God knows best, I find myself throwing in my opinions and conclusions.

When Evelyn Smith's case went to an administrative hearing, she was found guilty. In the judge's opinion, the state's right to protect unmarried couples overrode her rights to religious freedom. That is not the verdict I had in mind. But Mrs. Smith was undaunted.

"It's not over yet," she announced with confidence.

Nor is attorney Jordan Lorence discouraged. "Something much greater than real estate is at stake here," he told me. "What the state is saying is that a person can be punished for refusing to accommodate immorality. Even if we lose Mrs. Smith's case every step along the way—and that just may happen—I am committed to taking it all the way to the United States Supreme Court."

It is on this fifth level that a person really begins to *talk* to the Lord, to share the concerns of others and, in a selfless way, our own concerns. We don't just talk with God in our closet, nor do we limit ourselves to a set prayer time. We converse with Him constantly. For at this level, prayer is not just a separate activity. It is a continual, moment-by-moment thinking and breathing prayer. Level five comes when a person knows Christ on a level so deeply personal that He becomes a part of everything that person does and thinks and experiences.

Certainly no one reaches this fifth level of communication overnight. It comes from walking with the Lord and developing a most personal, intimate relationship with Him. And once we do achieve level five, we don't automatically stay there. We must work to maintain this intimate relationship.

On which communication level are you with God? Are you still reciting clichés or listing information to the Lord? Is your prayer time filled with telling God how He should be running things? My challenge to you is to move out of those impersonal stages and on into a deeper, more intimate time with Him. Once you do, you will never want to go back. I can guarantee it!

CHAPTER
6

FEAR CAN BLOCK GOD'S POWER

In the early days of Tim's and my ministry, I was terribly fear-prone. Unfortunately, many of my early decisions were based on the emotion of fear.

One day my husband announced he wanted to take flying lessons. In horror I said, "You mean you want to fly an airplane with only *one engine?*"

"Yes," he said, "that's what I'd be starting off with. What do you think?"

Well, I already had my mind made up. I said, "I think you're foolish! Why would you want to get into a plane with only one engine? What if something goes wrong? You won't have a spare!"

Tim asked me to pray about it. He wouldn't take the lessons, he assured me, unless I agreed, because I would have to make some sacrifices. First there would be a sacrifice of time—Tim would have to be gone a lot more for cross-country flights, ground school training and just logging the necessary hours for a license. Second—and even worse—the day would come when he would want me to fly with him.

"Of course I'll pray about it," I told Tim.

Well, I did pray. Over and over I begged, "Lord, you know how foolish this flying thing is. It's just too dangerous for Tim. Please change his heart. Take the desire to fly away from him."

I'm sure by now you've recognized that I was firmly stuck on that third level of prayer. Fear does that to us. And so I started right off giving God my opinions and drawing my own conclusions. My fear and anxiety was controlling me.

Tim's desire to fly turned out to be one of the major turning points of my life. One day my dear husband, who knows me well, said to me, "Honey, I know you've been praying about the flying lessons. But, I wonder, have you asked God to perhaps change *your* attitude?"

That took me aback. I thought, *What does he mean? I'm not the one who needs to change! I'm praying for him to change.*

"Be open with the Lord," Tim told me. "Share your heart and fears with Him. Let Him know you're afraid of flying, but that you're willing to be changed if that's what He would have."

And that's just what I did. I prayed, "Lord, I still think I'm right about Tim's flying, but if I'm the one who needs to be changed, then I'm ready for You to change my attitude and my fears."

All along, my own conclusion had steadfastly been that God needed to change Tim's heart. But my dread of Tim's being hurt—or even killed—in an accident didn't abate until I got to the point where I was willing to say, "Lord, if it's *my* heart that needs to be changed, then change me."

Over my obstinate resistance, God did just that. He changed me!

Tim took those flying lessons. Every time he went up for a lesson, I prayed and prayed, and over and over I committed him to the Lord. During the following months I developed a very warm prayer life with God on my husband's behalf!

Then came the day when Tim walked into the house and said, "Okay, Honey, I've got enough hours logged up now that you can fly with me. I'd like to take you up this afternoon."

Suddenly there was a whole different picture on my prayers. Now it wasn't just a matter of committing Tim to the Lord. I had to commit *Beverly* into God's hands, too. It was time to say, "I'll get into that plane with only one engine, Lord, and I'll fly in it because I know I'm in Your care." But I didn't come easily to that point. Again, my fear got in the way.

I thought of every possible reason why I couldn't go in the plane with Tim that day. "I'm right in the middle of doing the laundry and I have to finish it," I said.

But Tim was persistent. "All that will wait," he said. "Come and get in the car. I want to take you up right now while the weather's good."

In the end, I went. But all the way out to the airport, I thought, *Please, oh please, couldn't we delay this?* I finally prayed, *Please, God, help me to have the same peace to get in that plane as you gave me for Tim to fly.*

Well, we got to the airport and everything was fine. The mechanics had thoroughly checked out that single engine and fueled the gas tank. The sky was as clear and blue as could be—not a single cloud in sight. Together Tim and I walked toward the little plane. Tim showed me how to climb aboard and strap myself in. But every step of the way I kept on pleading, *Oh, Lord, is this what You really want?*

Tim turned the engine over and carefully checked off his check lists. Everything went perfectly. We taxied out to the end of the runway, and as Tim was revving up the engine, before he got the clearance to move on down the runway and take off, in desperation I reminded the Lord, *This is Your last chance! Is this what You want? If You do, You are really going to have to come through and carry me in Your arms because this is too frightening for me!*

Well, the Lord didn't stop the plane. We went on down the runway and took off—a beautiful take off, by the way. It was as if the Lord reached out and put His arms underneath the plane and carried us along.

As we went upward, I remember feeling so very close to the Lord. All of a sudden it became a spiritual experience. Just my husband and me in that little craft high up in the air, supported by God's loving arms underneath.

And you know what? After all my doubting and pleading and begging, I found myself actually enjoying the flight. There truly is an exhilaration in flying, more so in a small plane with all the gusts of wind and the characteristic sounds of the engine than in a big commercial plane.

When a few little gusts of wind came and

blew us around a bit, I anxiously asked, "What was that?" My first thought was that the engine might be having problems.

"It's nothing," Tim said. "Just a little wind." Comforted, I went right back to the realization that God's everlasting arms were under me.

I must admit that I didn't exactly jump into the plane with great excitement to make the second flight. Or the third or the fourth. But even when I was nervous to fly, I forced myself to go. And every time I flew, it got a little easier.

You know what? Flying turned out to be a wonderful experience for me. Forced to face my fears, I learned to trust God to lift me above them. I had to ask myself, "Okay, Beverly, is God able to take care of you or not?" I knew He was, since He'd already helped me to overcome the crippling effects of my arthritis. The next logical question was, "So, then, can you totally commit yourself to His care, or can't you?" Of course, I knew I could. The witness of His walking beside me during those hard months when I prepared myself to spend the rest of my life as an invalid proved that He could carry me through any fearful experience.

THE WITNESS OF PAST MEMORIES

Often when I'm fearful, I practice the art of reviewing the past, something taught to us by the patriarchs of the Bible. It is, in fact, a practice still employed by Jews throughout the world. I think about what has happened before in my life and review the ways God has helped me through other situations. I always try to remember one or two specific events in my life, such as my struggle with arthritis, and to recall the singular feeling of peace and joy I experienced as my fingers straightened out enough that I could once again comb my hair or sign my name.

Moses' last instructions to the Israelite people were to remember. "Remember how God led you out of Egypt." "Remember the way He parted the Red Sea." "Remember how He provided manna for you in the dry desert wilderness." "Remember . . ."

. . . and once a year, he told them, "Celebrate!" Celebrate God's blessing at the feast of the Passover. Spend a whole evening reviewing God's provision for you in the past and enjoying that memory together. "For by strength of hand the Lord has brought you out of this place" (Ex. 13:3). Moses reminded the Israelites, who often forgot—as we all seem to do—God's past blessing whenever they were faced with new hardships (Ex. 13:3).

Likewise, Christians need to remember and to celebrate. Throughout the year, when we are tempted to fall into the sin of fearfulness, we need to remember God's blessings of the past. No other testimony can be greater to us because those experiences are sure evidence of God's hand at work in our lives.

And once a year, why not have a celebration of your own? New Year's Eve has always been an uncomfortable holiday for me. There's an awful lot of false happiness in those scenes of dancing and drinking and wearing silly hats and blowing noisemakers and hugging and kissing people you barely know. What about a feast of New Year's Eve instead? Together your family can remember the ways in which God has provided for them in the past. Or, if the children have other activities, perhaps it might just be Mom and Dad. Certainly the two of you know what a miracle it is that God has brought you through a certain number of years of providing food and shelter and some amount of comfort for you and your children. You also know how miraculous it is that God has managed to protect you from your own weaknesses—fear or worry or anger or lust. Maybe this is a good time to look at family photo albums or films or videos and remember the past year—or years— this way.

God used Tim's desire to fly an airplane as a blessing in my life. Today, I celebrate that blessing. For it was in that experience more than any other that God taught me to lay my fears before Him and move forward in faith and power. 2 Timothy 1:7, "For God has not given us a spirit of fear, but of power and of love and of a sound mind." Fear will limit our experiencing the power of prayer.

God doesn't need my counsel. He doesn't depend on me to tell Him whose heart to change or which action is wise and which is foolish. What He does desire is for me to look to Him and be open to His direction. And He wishes me to be willing to change the way He is leading me to change.

My battle with fear began years before that airplane ride. I've always battled fear of one sort or another—fear of failure, fear of opposition, fear that I wouldn't be accepted, fear of new situations. I was naturally a fearful person. And little did I realize that the victory over fear of flying was a stepping stone to prepare me for greater service for Him in the future.

FEAR OF FAILURE

My husband and I started our life together involved in the local church. Because Tim was a pastor, I was immediately thrown into leadership. There I was, a young, fearful woman with a very poor self-image, pushed into playing the part of a skillful and capable pastor's wife.

The women looked to me to be a leader. I was expected to teach Bible classes, to play the organ, lead the choir, to stand up and pray eloquently in public, to bake the very best cakes—all this was, I thought, part of my new job description. Suddenly, I found myself thrust into an area in which I felt I was totally inadequate.

Instead of trying to sharpen up and meet these challenges and expectations, I retreated. Where I started out lacking confidence, I became downright fearful. And the more fearful I became, the more intimidated I felt.

During the early years of our ministry, I remember agreeing to give a devotional even though I was scared to death. A few weeks later one of the ladies shared with me that I had not done a very good job and I needed to work on a few things before ever doing it again. This was more than my already poor self-image could handle, so after that when I was asked, I responded, "My husband is the speaker in the family. I'm just his helpmeet." At the time I thought this was an adequate answer. But when I look back on it now, I'm really ashamed of myself. I was hiding behind Tim's ministerial coat and trying to excuse myself for fear of failing again.

One day I was abruptly brought face-to-face with what I was doing. We had been in the ministry fifteen or sixteen years. Throughout that time I had limited myself to teaching young children in Sunday school; only with them did I feel comfortable. Then one day Dr. Henry Brandt took me aside and pointed out 2 Timothy 1:7: "For God has not given us a spirit of fear, but of power and of love and of a sound mind." Then, without trying to spare my feelings, he told me, "Beverly, your fear is based on selfishness and that is a sin. You need to deal with it."

A sin! I was staggered.

Dr. Brandt didn't stop there. "Beverly," he told me, "You're all wrapped up with fear and a poor self-image, and that is caused by selfishness."

Believe me, this was not easy to hear! But it was the best thing in the world for me. And when Dr. Brandt started repeating my own words back to me, just as I'd said them to him, I could see it all. It was obvious even to me.

FEAR IS A SIN

Few of us think of fear as a sin. Yet in the next days as I thought about Dr. Brandt's words and read the Scriptures, I realized he was right. I might not be committing murder or stealing or cheating on my husband, but I *was* committing a sin.

In Romans 14:23, the apostle Paul tells us, "for whatever is not from faith is sin." God wants us to walk by faith. But fear is not from faith, therefore fear is sin.

To see the contrast between faith and fear, let's take a look at Daniel. Coerced by governors jealous of Daniel, King Darius signed his name to a royal decree that anyone caught praying to any god or man for the next thirty days would be cast into a den of hungry lions.

Daniel knew all about the law, and he knew the penalty for breaking it. Now, I don't know about you, but if I were faced with a den of hungry lions, I think I would pray in my closet for the next month. God could hear me just as well from there, I'd reason. Besides, what good would I be to God as a lion's main course?

Well, that's not the way Daniel saw it. He went straight up to his room, and in front of his window open toward Jerusalem, he knelt down and prayed to God—out loud. He had done this three times every day of his life, and he wasn't about to change his worship habits now.

Well, you know the story. Daniel was caught in the trap laid by the jealous governors, and there was nothing King Darius could do to help him. But he knew all about Daniel and his faith in God, so even as Daniel was cast into the lion's den, the king said to him, "Your God, whom you serve continually, He will deliver you." I'm not sure the king actually believed it, but Daniel certainly did.

Very early the next morning, the king jumped from his bed and ran to the den of lions. "Daniel, servant of the living God," he called out, "has your God been able to deliver you from the lions?"

From the depths of the den came Daniel's voice, strong and fearless. "O king," he called, "my God sent His angel and shut the lion's mouths. They have not hurt me because I am innocent."

How could Daniel be so fearless? Because of his faith. Faith and fear don't mix. And whatever is not of faith is sin.

All those years God knew my heart. He knew I really wanted to be a godly woman. It was just that I didn't know how to pull myself out of that fearful crippling self-doubt.

The day that Dr. Brandt spoke with me, I began a long struggle to rebuild my life. Actually it was more a matter of allowing the Holy Spirit to do the rebuilding. I began to pray for a way to overcome the fear that was destroying me. I needed to stop controlling my own life with the fearful emotions and allow the Holy Spirit to take control. In answer to that prayer, He immediately began to show me the way—not all at once, but step by step.

As I look back in retrospect, I think I was actually pulling my husband down as well because I was always kind of a wet blanket for him. If he offered, "Should we do this?" or "Do you think we should try that?" I always had a reason why we shouldn't or why it would never work.

I dealt with my fear of failure, but other fears still cowered inside me. I didn't know that, but God did, and in the years that followed He helped me to see those other lurking fears.

FEAR OF OPPOSITION

At Concerned Women for America, I came to the place where I had to be very honest with the Lord. I had to tell Him how really afraid I was to do what I was convinced He was calling me to do. I'd see Eleanor Smeal and Betty Friedan on television, raising their clenched fists high, screaming out in shrill voices, and I was convinced that God meant for someone else to do this job instead of me.

Now, I am a peaceful woman. I don't like conflict. It's important to me that people like me. It is not my nature to enter such a combative, militant arena. As I watched and listened to the women I knew we had to oppose, I questioned God's leading, and yet God had led me to take a stand for righteousness.

Very quickly I learned that it's not possible to remain fearful and still take a firm stand for righteousness. You can pray for God to protect your family and other families in our land, but you can't take that next step—you can't pray and then *act*—if you are bound by the sin of fear.

Standing for righteousness carries a price tag. In that position one doesn't have the luxury of carefully looking at each situation and weighing it, then asking, "Should I or shouldn't I?" If I were truly going to take a stand for righteousness, I had no choice but to march right in and say, "By God's grace, I *will* do this!" "I can do all things through Christ who strengthens me" (Phil. 4:13).

And so, praying a prayer expressing my fears became a very personal experience. Of course, God already knew my fears. I realized He didn't have to be apprised of them. But for me to learn to express them to Him was a necessary step; as I talked them over with God and asked Him for help in overcoming, I began to recognize and verbalize each fear.

Many times I prayed back to God that Scripture that Dr. Brandt had given me: "For God has not given us a spirit of fear, but of power and of love and of a sound mind." Many times as I spoke out against the deception taught by Eleanor Smeal or Molly Yard or some other feminist leader, my mind clung tightly to that scriptural promise.

Today, at this phase of my work with CWA, I am sometimes criticized. Again and again I am confronted by people who don't like me, and occasionally I get "hate" letters in the mail. Sometimes I even get threats. Without God, my natural fearfulness would rise up and shout, "Enough of this! I'm getting out of here. I'm going back home where I'm loved and secure and comfortable!"

Yet God built a protective shield around me. I'm convinced it is because my prayer has been that, more than anything else, God would enable me to do what He wants me to do—even if it means getting hate letters and having people not like me. In the end, you see, what people think of me isn't really important. What *is* important is that I be obedient to the Lord Jesus Christ—even when I dislike opposition and even when I'm afraid of not being in control. This, you see, is yet another kind of fear God has helped me to overcome.

FEAR OF NOT BEING IN CONTROL

Sometimes the worst fear of all is the fear of not being in control. In 1987 I was asked to appear in a panel of six people on a segment of Oprah Winfrey's talk show. The subject was advertising condoms on television. Three panelists were in favor of such advertising and three, including me, were against it.

Now, I can tell you, the subject of condoms is one I'd prefer not to discuss at all. Ten years ago I never dreamed I'd be talking about such a thing in mixed company, let alone on national television! Yet the time may come when we have to take on subjects we'd just as soon ignore. This was one of those times. I felt so strongly about my position that I knew I should be there to represent and support it.

Before I agreed to appear on the show, I specifically asked if any condoms would be shown. (Since I was opposed to condoms on television, to have them displayed right there would, I felt, be working against me.) When the production personnel assured me there wouldn't be any, I said, "Okay, then I'll participate on the panel."

As the show started, each panelist had a turn to speak and make specific points. All was going fine when Oprah paused for a commercial break, then left to take a break herself.

We didn't know it, but the two front rows in the studio were filled with homosexuals who had flown in to Chicago from San Francisco. During the commercial break they went out and brought back a big box.

Then they proceeded to hand out bags to everyone in the audience as well as to us on the platform. When they handed one to me, I refused to take it. It was as if the Lord whispered to me, "Don't take that. If you do, you're going to get caught with the goods in your hands!" Things happened so fast that I didn't even have time to pray. Still, I sensed the Lord guiding my actions and reactions.

The bags were marked "Safe Sex Kits."

The young woman on the other end of the panel proudly admitted that she had "starred" in a pornographic film that displayed "safe sex" techniques. During a commercial break, she opened her little bag and pulled out a condom and some rubber gloves. She thought it was hilarious. She put on the gloves, making jokes the whole time.

We brought the kits to Oprah's attention and she tried to explain their appearance on the show. Those of us against condom advertising protested loudly. After the program began again, I told Oprah with the cameras rolling, "We came on this show to talk about why we objected to condoms being advertised on television and you've already done it. It's been on television now. I'm really offended by this."

"There aren't any condoms here," Oprah said.

"Look around," I told her. "Everyone here has a bag with several condoms in it."

Oprah was astounded. She had no idea what was going on.

"I want you to know I am offended and terribly disappointed that this show has deteriorated to such a low level," I told her.

The Lord gave me the push to say those words at just that moment. It was something I would never have had the courage to say myself.

But from that point on, the show got more and more out of hand. Oprah totally lost control. I really believe in my heart that if she could have pulled the plug on that show that day, she would have done it in a minute.

One by one the homosexuals spoke into the mike and preached about how we "fundamentalist Christians" are so narrow and insist that everyone else live by our rules.

I don't blame Oprah for what happened. The homosexual contingent were well organized. They knew exactly what they were doing. They were in favor of advertising condoms on television, and they accomplished their goal. Without a doubt, condoms were being advertised loudly and clearly right there that day.

A situation that would have produced great fear in the past was instead, a position of strength and courage. God was faithful and provided the power and sound mind that was promised.

When we walk with God, when we pray first and then act, we will move in God's strength and become all He wants us to be. Way back there in California, so many years ago, God saw Beverly LaHaye a lot differently than I saw myself. Day by day, step by step, He's moved me toward His own vision of the person I am and am to become.

THE WONDERFUL CONSEQUENCE OF CONFRONTING YOUR FEAR

When God confronted me with my fear of flying in a one-engine airplane, I had no idea He would later take Tim and me into areas of the world where we would have to fly in just such a plane. From deep in the jungles of Mexico where Wycliffe trains missionaries, to a little isolated mission village in New Guinea, we ministered to missionaries and their families. Later, I began to make frequent trips into the jungles of Costa Rica to work among the Nicaraguan refugees, and now recently into the interior of Nicaragua, even though I was well aware that the danger of an emergency landing in those remote areas is far greater than in California.

When Tim decided to take those long-ago flying lessons, I never dreamed what was to come. But God knew. And He was preparing me. Had He said way back then, "Okay Beverly, today you've got to pass this test because in twenty years I'm going to have you flying into the jungle right up to the Nicaraguan border in a little plane with just one engine," I couldn't have done it.

None of what God has opened the doors for me to do today would have been possible if I had failed that test back then. But God didn't tell me that. He led me along one step at a time.

Three years ago, Tim and I were flying in a little eighteen passenger commuter plane with one of our attorneys when a turbulent storm blew up. As the sky outside grew darker and more ominous, that little plane bounced and tossed around in the air. Our attorney is not a fearful man, but he was terrified that day. He told me he bowed his head and began confessing every sin he ever committed. Then he begged God to take care of his family after he was gone.

When he opened his eyes, he says, he looked over at Tim and me. Tim was writing away, not at all concerned about the storm. I was sound asleep.

"I don't get it," he told me later. "How could you sleep so peacefully with that terrible storm going on outside?"

"It has to be God," I told him. "Only He could have brought me from that crippling fearfulness I once had to a place where I could fly through such a storm and still be at peace."

How about you? Is there fear or anxiety in your life that are limiting what God can do? Have you admitted that fear to the Lord? Have you asked Him to help you overcome it? Prayer is your weapon against fear. Prayer is the key that opens a reservoir of power for you.

God is moving you one step at a time toward becoming all you can be. I doubt that you can begin to imagine all He has in store for you. I know I couldn't!

CHAPTER
7

UNITED IN PRAYER ACROSS THE NATION

I t was 1979. Betty Friedan, spokeswoman for the National Organization for Woman (NOW), was proclaiming "We speak for the women of America!"

Well, she surely wasn't speaking for me. And I know a good many other women for whom she wasn't speaking, either.

The original idea behind Concerned Women for America was that Christian women also need to be heard. We knew that wasn't going to happen unless we could rally our traditionally silent side together and speak with a united voice.

In 1980 I went to a luncheon at which Vonette Bright spoke on prayer. "We should never attempt anything for God without first thoroughly saturating it in prayer," she said.

The Lord heavily impressed upon me that Concerned Women for America was entering an arena that had to be undergirded with prayer.

On the way home from the luncheon another of our CWA board members who had gone with me, said, "Beverly, you know today when Vonette spoke, I felt like she was talking to us." We both agreed that prayer would have to be a necessary part of this young growing organization. That day was the launching of our prayer chapters which have become the source of strength for CWA.

Unexpectedly, and without much preparation, we were finding ourselves thrown into progressively bigger, more important issues. The situations in which we were becoming involved were staggering. In the past, my fears of failure and opposition would have destroyed me, but God was fulfilling in my life just what He had promised. He was the source of power.

On some days, I wasn't at all sure I'd be able to tackle some of the tough issues that loomed ahead of us. Now, at last, I saw the missing element. What we were lacking was powerful, organized prayer support.

We as a board agreed that prayer was our secret to success. Many ladies could be involved all over the country. One board member added, "Prayer chapters in every state who pray first, then act would make us uniquely different from any other organization."

THE POWER OF PRAYER/ACTION CHAPTERS

Our first attempt at large-scale, organized prayer came in the form of prayer chains made up of seven women each. Our procedure was to contact the first lady on each chain. She called lady number two, lady number two called lady number three, and so on down through the chain. Lady number seven mailed a card that said, "The chain has been completed." When those cards came back to us, we knew another seven women were backing us daily in prayer. What a thrill it was to get those cards and know the women were praying!

The response was immediate. People from all over America wrote to us asking to be part of a chain. Here, finally, was something they could do.

Before we really had time to get ourselves organized, the Equal Rights Amendment was thrust upon us. The ERA was the big subject of the day. Because it was to be an amendment to the United States Constitution, it had to be voted on state by state. When it came up for a vote in the state of Illinois, someone who worked with Phyllis Schlafly called me and said, "We're exhausted! All of our people have worked long hours and just cannot do any more. Is there any way you can help us?"

To be honest, we weren't in much of a position to help them. I was naive and none of us knew much about the political process. We were still only a small group of no more than eighteen hundred women with a core group of just five women in San Diego directing out limited endeavors. What we did know how to do, however, was pray. And so in prayer our board asked, "What can we do, Lord, that would help back there in Illinois?"

As though in answer to our prayer, we were approached with this request: "Could CWA put together some professional sixty-second commercials we could run on television?" What the organizers had in mind were spots that would simply state why a woman didn't want to have this kind of amendment controlling her life.

We agreed to do so.

The plan was to produce four different spots, each one a quality piece. Then we would purchase 120 segments of television air time in Springfield, the state capital of Illinois. For an entire week before the vote, we would saturate the city with the spots. We didn't yet know the cost, though we did know the project wouldn't come cheap. We alerted our prayer chains. Then we waited for God's help and strength so that we could take action.

Tim and I were speaking at a Home Interiors management conference in the mountains of Colorado when I got a call from our office in San Diego saying, "The cost for the television spots will be forty-five thousand dollars." As I stood in shocked silence, he added, "If we are to have this ready in time, we've got to get to work on it immediately. I need your decision by tomorrow."

We were a small organization just starting out. We didn't have a big membership supporting us. We were just a group of Christian women determined to stand up for righteousness. Where were we going to get forty-five thousand dollars?

I left that phone call and arrived back at the meeting just as our hostess, Mary Crowley, was introducing Tim to speak. I must have had a troubled look on my face, for Mary pulled me aside and said, "Is there anything I can pray about regarding that phone call?"

"Oh, Mary," I told her, "you won't believe what's happening. I've never been in such a spot before." Then I told her all about the television spots and our decision that had to be made in a few hours and the forty-five thousand dollars we didn't have.

"I don't know what to tell you," she said quite honestly. "We'd better pray." And that's exactly what we did.

After Tim finished speaking, Mary went up to the platform and explained to the audience what was happening. "First we're going to pray," she said, "then we're going to pass a basket around for any of you who want to help. You certainly don't have to give. But for those of you who want to, we'll take an offering of both money and pledges."

That day, from that assembly, Mary Crowley raised the entire forty-five thousand dollars we needed to do those commercials!

I could hardly believe what had happened. That day I finally began to comprehend the power of a concerned group united in prayer. I called the agent and told him to go ahead with the project.

Those sixty-second spots aired all week before the ERA vote. You could hardly turn on the television in the Illinois state capital without seeing one of them. The project was effective.

It was at this time, when we were so involved in the Equal Rights Amendment fight, that our dependence on our prayer chapters became particularly apparent to us. And our praying members rose to the occasion.

137

During the last few months of the ERA battle, we designated every Wednesday at noon as an hour for the prayer chapters to pray for each state that was to be voting on the ERA. And in state after state we watched in awe as the amendment was defeated. We saw miracle after miracle after miracle unfold before our eyes.

We really needed to see those victories back then, for those miraculous successes reinforced us in the certainty that God was indeed leading us. And they proved to us the power of prayer.

The day the Illinois vote was to take place, I led CWA's little team of our women to the state capitol where we held a press conference.

A huge contingent of NOW women had come from all over the United States, sleeping bags in tow. They had set up loud speakers in the capitol and positioned themselves in the immense rotunda. The entire rotunda was filled with several hundred women, all singing songs mostly derogatory about men. They looked at the four of us from CWA with obvious hostility and contempt. Four against several hundred! The odds certainly were in their favor. It was interesting how few of them gave the appearance of being mothers. If they were, it was well disguised.

I thought, *Lord, are you SURE this is where you want me? Is this really what you want me to do? Could I possibly have misunderstood you?* You can believe I questioned the Lord that day! Yet there was a growing confidence and peace that God was there directing our steps.

I had never been involved in a press conference before. Pastors' wives don't hold press confer-
ences. I hardly knew what to do. Quickly I was briefed,
then again and again I went over the statement I had
written out. We were joined by two or three other ladies
and one gentleman who were state representatives and
who would be voting against the ERA in a few days. I'll
have to admit I was gripped with fear. And yet I kept
telling myself that God had raised all the money for the
television project. He had led us each step of the way, so
surely He was not going to leave us now.

As the press conference began, about six
feminists had entered the room, distinctively dressed in
green and white tee shirts with National Organization
for Women slogans emblazoned across them. The
women had tried to intimidate us and would have liked
to break up our press conference. But all over the country, people were appealing to God on our behalf. God
heard those prayers, and He prevented the disruption.

That night the feminists held an all-night sit-
in right there in the capitol. Hundreds of women banded
together—singing songs, exchanging slanderous slogans, and waving insulting banners. They were anything but feminine. It was a terrifying sight to behold. In
order to frighten and intimidate the state representatives who would soon be voting, they poured animal
blood across the marble floor of the capital rotunda. The
threat wasn't lost on any of us: Come election day, the
political blood of any legislator who dared vote against
ERA would likewise be spilt.

When the vote was taken the next morning,

the Equal Rights Amendment went down in defeat in Illinois. It was a success for "prayer, then action."

That day we realized how important it was that we get many more prayer chapters in operation immediately. And that's just what we did.

PRAYER/ACTION CHAPTERS EMERGE

Three major objectives of Concerned Women for America are to inform women in our country of the erosion of our historical Judeo-Christian moral standards, to expose to them movements seeking to weaken the family, and to educate women in the principles for living as laid out in the Word of God. All three of these activities contribute toward an all-important fourth goal: to organize a nationwide prayer network. To be most effective, this network must be composed of strong individual units. It is these units that we call prayer/action chapters.

Let me give you an idea how these chapters work. Each one has a leader, who must first make application and be approved by her CWA "Area Representative." This leader serves as the contact person for the Area Representative and passes along prayer and action alerts to the chapter members. The leader is responsible for keeping the members informed with prayer information and with action assignments.

Although we suggest various plans for organizing chapters, we leave the final arrangements up to the chapter leader and the Area Representative. What works well in a chapter meeting at a church may not be so successful in a neighborhood chapter, a business office chapter, or an evening couples' chapter. The best plan, we have discovered, is the plan that works for that specific group. As you can see, our organized prayer groups have changed over the years! (For more information about prayer/action chapters, see the appendix.)

When an important event such as the Illinois press conference comes up today, we send out an alert to all our prayer/action chapter leaders. We might say: "We're going to be having a press conference at the Illinois state capitol. We're going to be there face-to-face with the opposition, so we need you to be praying for us." Or, we might say. "This week we will be on "Donahue," "Good Morning America," etc., and we want you to pray specifically for these things . . ."

This approach has made all the difference in the world. Now we are able to face such a situation in quiet confidence. Even though opposition appears to be strong, even though the numbers in the polls are always against us, we have a quiet confidence that "greater is He who is in us than he who is in the world."

Very quickly we had a chance to put our prayer/action chapters to work. Our next involvement was in the White House Conference on Families here in Washington, D.C. My husband and I joined a little coalition that was going to try to do something to oppose a group attempting to change the definition of a family to include such perverse groups as homosexual couples.

To counteract the national liberal emphasis, we put together a conference on our own in the Long Beach Auditorium. We brought in all the pro-family

141

speakers we knew of. Over seven thousand people attended. That conference had a major impact on holding back the flood of misinformation aimed at changing the definition of the American family and maintaining the traditional values of the family.

All during this time our organized prayer support continued to grow. We kept our chapter members assessed on what was going on, and they were faithful in their commitment to pray. There truly was power in that united prayer!

So far, those prayer/action chapters had not been involved in many battles of their own. But in 1988, one of the prayer/action chapters found itself fighting its own equal access lawsuit.

A PRAYER/ACTION CHAPTER FIGHTS ITS OWN BATTLES

Our prayer chapter in Oxford, Mississippi, decided to hold its meetings at a neutral site, one that would be comfortable to all members regardless of their religious background. So chapter leader Jolene Cox asked permission to use the meeting room of the local library.

"The librarian told me no, that religious groups weren't allowed to meet there," says Jolene.

When Jolene asked just what constituted a religious group, she was told that if they were going to pray at their meetings, they were considered a religious group.

"You mean, if we didn't pray we could meet here in the library, but since we pray, we can't?" Jolene asked in disbelief.

"That's right," she was told.

Jolene was appalled. As a taxpayer, she helped support that library. What right did they have to bar her group from using it just because they chose to exercise their freedom to pray?

"It just wasn't right!" Jolene says.

That very evening Jolene called CWA attorney Jordan Lorence. When contacted by Jordan, the regional director of the library told him the prayer chapter meetings would be a violation of their policy. If the board were to allow prayer in the library, he insisted, they would be violating the Constitution.

"Not so," Jordan informed him. "By allowing everybody to come in except religious groups, what you are doing is violating the free speech rights of these Concerned Women for America members."

Some people insist it's foolish to go to court over something such as this. Certainly it wasn't an easy decision for Jolene Cox, especially when some of her own prayer chapter members encouraged her to drop it.

"We really prayed about it," Jolene says. "You can't take someone to court just to be taking them to court. God wouldn't honor that."

Jolene Cox and Jordan Lorence tried every possible avenue to work out the situation before they took the step of filing suit against the library. Nothing worked. Jordan explained to Jolene that barring access to public buildings is by no means limited to libraries. Nor did the discrimination touch just this one prayer chapter. In the long run a decision on the Mississippi case could touch the life of every Christian in the United States who desires to pray.

"In the end, it was this point that convinced me to go ahead with the suit," Jolene explains. "Jordan helped me see that it isn't just a little case here in Oxford, Mississippi. It can have far-reaching effects."

To be able to pray freely and unhampered is one of our fundamental freedoms. Americans have been so intimidated that many no longer know what's factual and what isn't. For instance most people believe a person can't legally bow her head before lunch or whisper a prayer before a geometry test in school. That isn't so. It's time Americans realize just what their rights are.

After prayerful consideration, Concerned Women for America filed an equal access suit on behalf of Jolene Cox and the CWA prayer chapter.

In equal access cases, when our attorneys meet with the attorneys for the other side, our attorneys begin by informing the opposing attorneys of the government officials that, according to the law, if other groups are allowed to meet in a public place, a religious group cannot be denied access simply because of the content of their speech. Often they respond, "Really? Is that true? I didn't realize that!" Then they say, "We're sorry. Your group can certainly meet here," and the matter is dropped.

But the Oxford library's official response was, "I don't care what the Supreme Court says. You can't meet here, and that's that!"

We knew we were in for a battle, so we alerted our prayer chapters and asked them to pray.

When the case went to trial, the judge agreed with everything our attorneys said. The library had no right to ban the prayer chapter, he ruled.

The library responded with an appeal. Again we committed ourselves to prayer, and again we asked our constituents to do the same. As is customary, three federal appeals court judges were to be drawn at random to hear our case, so we prayed specifically that God would cause the right judges to be chosen.

One week before the trial, the CWA attorneys learned who the three judges were who would hear the appeal.

Two of the judges were the ones they were certain would be most sympathetic to our side. The other judge they weren't so sure about.

The library presented its side first. Almost before the words were hardly out of the attorney's mouth, the judge we were most concerned about spoke up. "I can't believe you're making those kinds of arguments!" he said. "They lack merit." Then another judge jumped in. "You people are attacking the free speech of these ladies! How dare you have a policy like this?"

It was obvious that those judges had nothing but contempt for the library's position. In the end, they wrote a 3–0 opinion that totally agreed with every point we had argued. Their decision applied to the state of Mississippi, Louisiana, and Texas.

That day, in answer to the prayers of many, many people across the nation, God allowed Jolene Cox's equal access suit against the library in Oxford, Mississippi, to demonstrate clearly and decisively that Christians are not to be discriminated against because they pray. We are protected by the Constitution of the United States.

During the appeal, Jolene had to travel from

Mississippi to New Orleans. Two other CWA members went along simply to sit in the courtroom and pray—for Jolene, for our attorneys, for the three judges trying the case, and that God's purpose would ultimately be accomplished through the trial.

God honored those prayers. The prayer chapter is now meeting in the library.

"If I were ever to find out that just one person came to know the Lord because some group got to meet in a building as a result of our suit, it would make the whole thing worthwhile," Jolene Cox says.

Even if she never has that satisfaction, Jolene and all of us who supported her in prayer have no doubt that God directed the case. He saw it through step by step, and He alone knows what ultimate results may come from that decision.

"There were some high school students in Texas who wanted to hold a prayer meeting before school," Jolene says. "It became a big issue. Now, I can't say for sure what the direct influence was, but the school's attorney referred to our Mississippi judgment that had just been handed down. 'Look' they told the school officials, 'because of the recent verdict of the federal appeals court, we think you've got to let these students hold their prayer meeting.'"

We don't know how many places will refer to that decision and say, "These people have an equal right to these facilities." But we do know God answered our prayer.

146

NOTIFYING MEMBERS OF PRAYER CONCERNS

A full page in our newsletter is devoted to our prayer/action network. The order of items replicates the order of prayer. First *praise* (as demonstrated by this item in our November/December 1989 issue):

For the victories in the Tampa, Florida, and Oxford, Mississippi, equal access cases. [Jolene Cox's prayer/action group was the Mississippi case.]

Then *prayer* (this from the same issue):

For CWA attorneys as they prepare for oral arguments in the Ken Roberts Bible censorship case in Denver on January 18. Pray for wisdom and spiritual might during the trial.

Finally, *action:*

All Pennsylvanians can write your state representatives and let them know how pleased you are with the recent pro-life vote in the state House. Urge your legislators to continue protecting the rights of the pre-born.

By reading the prayer/action network page of our newsletters, every member of CWA is able to pray and act with factual information about the issues facing families across America. In addition, the local leadership is able to include many special requests that involve community, city, and state issues. One of the most common and oft reported requests is concerning their local school boards, principals, or curriculum.

THE KEY SIXTEEN

Another prayer emphasis we bring before our prayer groups is what we call the "Key Sixteen." This is a list of sixteen leaders who are in key positions in the government, people who make decisions that affect our lives every day. Besides the President and Vice President of the United States, this list includes the two senators, congressmen, the governor and the mayor from the group's area. It also includes the nine chief justices seated on the Supreme Court. We encourage our chapter members to pray continually for all sixteen of these key individuals.

Why do we put so much emphasis on our organized prayer groups? Because we know full well that without prayer—specific, ongoing, intercessory prayer—we can do nothing. And we know that the power of united group prayer cannot be measured.

After we have prayed for direction from the Lord and have done everything we can do, we must let go and place the matter in God's hands. How wonderful at such a time to know we have literally thousands of people in over fifteen hundred prayer chapters around the country joining us in prayer. Together we are calling upon God to move in and cause something divine to happen, something far beyond anything possible through our own limited human capabilities.

What a lot has happened in CWA! When

Concerned Women for America was first established, never in my wildest imagination did I dream we'd come so far. Back then my only aim was to have the Lord use me in my own little county of San Diego, California. All I wanted to do was alert the women of our local churches about what was happening in our country. But after we got going, when we saw CWA starting to take off and grow, when Christian women started rallying to what we were doing, I began to realize we were holding onto something critical. We dared not continue on without strengthening our foundation—consistent, unified, concentrated prayer.

CWA has made incredible strides since those early days of the Equal Rights Amendment. Now we're involved in many things. We lobby for all types of matters that concern the family—matters such as abortion, education, pornography, and drugs. We also lobby on bills that focus on such things as child care and parental consent. In the courts we fight for First Amendment rights, parental rights, and religious freedom. We have given the Christian women in America an opportunity to stand up for righteousness and to let their voices be heard with a united influence. Add to these activities the humanitarian aid projects we conduct with the Nicaraguan refugees in Costa Rica and our own prayer chapters, and you will begin to get an idea of why we depend so heavily on our prayer support.

NOW has changed, too. No longer is this feminist group the militant, anti-men organization that poured the blood across the floor of the Illinois state capitol. What has not changed is NOW's agenda. The chasm between our two organizations is as deep as ever. Concerned Women for America is centered around the family, protecting unborn babies, and strengthening the role of motherhood. The National Organization for Women, on the other hand, is centered around concerns for themselves. Their agenda is based on *their* rights, *their* freedoms, *their* bodies. For them, everything is "me, me, me."

If we had a reason to organize for prayer back at our beginning, we have a far greater reason to do so now.

It's not easy to endure a legal case. Some cases we consider pivotal go through several appeals; then the defendant becomes so weary he or she just cannot go any further.

"All the sacrifices and humiliation, the depressing stories and the phone ringing off the hook, people writing to the newspaper, and people sending me nasty letters," Jolene Cox says with a sigh when she recalls her trial. Yet she insists her ordeal was nowhere near as trying as those which others have had to go through.

"I have a poster on my wall," Jolene says, "the same kind Ken Roberts had to take off his schoolroom wall in Colorado. Beside it I've taped a little note saying: 'Pray for Ken Roberts.' Every time I pass that poster I think about Ken and say a prayer for him because I know what he's going through."

The fact that most people do continue on, often all the way up to the Supreme Court, is a tribute to the faithful, persistent prayer of our chapter members. Many people tell us that.

Because so many of our cases are landmark cases, many of them are thoroughly covered by the media.

"When I read about those cases, I feel so strongly for those who are going through the court system," Jolene says. "That's why I have committed myself to pray for them every day."

The strength of our Prayer/Action Chapters is becoming a recognizing source of power and success. Recently, a pro-family organization called our office to ask if we would have our prayer chapters pray for a request they had. That is the kind of reputation we can be thankful for.

As you can see, the bedrock of CWA's work is the prayer/action chapters. That's why we have set a miraculous goal for the 1990s.

TEN THOUSAND PRAYER/ACTION GROUPS IN THE 1990S

We are pleased with the progress of our prayer chapters, but we are not satisfied. With the growing threat of the New Age movement, the curse of Satanism among our children, plus the anti-Christian bigotry on the rise, we cannot be content with the prayer strength we now have. Our goal is ten thousand active chapters operating nationally.

We need a greater prayer covering than ever before.

Second Chronicles 7:14 "If My people who are called by My name will humble themselves, and pray and seek My face, and turn from their wicked ways, then I will hear from heaven, and will forgive their sin and heal their land."

We need a greater emphasis on prayer. Sad, indeed is the fact that often the first service in the local church to be eliminated or substituted is the prayer meeting. It is time for God's people to humble themselves and pray and turn from sin. CWA would like to be a part of that exciting direction.

CHAPTER
8

SPEAKING BOLDLY TO SAVE OUR FAMILIES

Along with the faithful prayer support from CWA women came the need to become actively involved.

In Ephesians 6:18–19, we see a definite progression taking place: "praying always [step 1] with all prayer and supplication in the Spirit, being watchful [step 2] to this end with all perseverance and supplication for all the saints—and for me, that utterance may be given to me, that I may open my mouth boldly [step 3] to make known the mystery of the gospel" (NKJV).

The exhortation begins with the admonition to pray "always." Not only do we need to pray, but we need to keep it up. Then we are told to be "watchful." To me, to be watchful means to be informed—to make sure we know and understand what it is we're praying about. In verse nineteen, we are instructed to "speak boldly." It's here that the action comes in.

This progression is important. First, we are to pray. Then we are to make sure we understand what it is we're praying about. Without being informed we are at a loss as to how to pray specifically. After we have taken those first two steps, we are to get busy and do something about our prayer. We are to act. Without action we waste the valuable resource of our own influence.

We quickly found that once women get involved in serious prayer, they quickly begin to ask, "But what can I *do?*" Once a person gets a burden for praying, that burden is quickly translated into a desire to take action. That's the way it should be. That's how God intends us to respond: pray first, then act. God often uses those who carry the burden to also effect a change.

Our prayer/action chapters have a much wider function than simply providing prayer support. We now put a great emphasis on helping members understand the people and issues for whom they are praying and why each concern is important.

Most of our women, we have found, truly do want to do something constructive. The problem is, they often are not informed about political matters. And so they ask, "How can we find out more about these issues? And once we know, what can we do?"

One of our important functions, then, is to provide our members with clear, understandable information. We do the research, we gather the facts, and we give the information out to our chapter members. After they review it, they are able to pray knowledgeably and with insight. If there is a letter to be written, they are prepared to write an intelligent letter.

We regularly prepare position papers on each major legislative issue and send it out to congressional representatives to help educate them. Then we put together a short summary paper to send out to our prayer chapter leaders to educate and prepare them for prayer and action. In addition, the Area Representatives supply each leader with a list of issues in her state that need special prayer. The leaders pass the summary on to the women in their chapter, and they discuss it. Of course, they also add things that are going on in their own communities. Then, armed with information and facts, the women go to prayer, considering each issue specifically.

After the group has prayed, the leader takes out paper and pens and a list of addresses. While the issues are still fresh in their minds, the women take action—they write letters to their senators or representative. Or, if there are phone calls that need to be made, they now have at their fingertips the talking points to be discussed.

See why we call the groups prayer/action chapters?

It's amazing what can happen when Christians walk in God's strength to influence matters that affect the family. Prayer makes the difference. Sometimes major legislation is canceled or confusion develops within the anti-family forces. Individual lives are changed. We hear of CWA members throughout the country who are praying and acting on local and state issues every day. Let me tell you about two of them, a woman I will call Diane and a single parent named Betsy.

ONE WOMAN MAKES A DIFFERENCE

For some women, writing letters isn't enough involvement. Diane was one of those women.

Diane married a man with a couple of children. "What I married was a family," she says. An instant mother, Diane quickly became interested in matters that affect children. For the first time in her life she began to take seriously all that was happening in education and family issues.

When Diane first heard about CWA, she became involved enough to quickly discover how little she knew about how our government works. *Well,* she decided, *I'll just have to learn. If they're going to make decisions that affect my children, I want to know as much about it as I possibly can.*

Diane lived quite some distance from the state capital. She didn't know anyone who had ever actually gone down there and tried to find out what was happening. So she prayed. Then she talked the matter over with her husband, and together they spent time before the Lord. God answered Diane's prayer by laying it upon her heart to drive down to the state capital herself and see what she could find out.

Dawn had not yet broken when Diane left her home and started her drive down to the capital. On her way she wondered, *What can I do to make them notice me?* Just at that moment she saw someone selling flowers by the side of the road, so she stopped and bought some roses.

Every time she visited someone in the legislature, Diane decided, she would give that person a rose. That way the person would know—and maybe even remember—who she was.

Diane's reception was gratifying. One legislator told her right out, "If you represent NOW or a group like it, don't even bother coming back to my office. I don't have the time."

"Oh, no," Diane told him. "I represent people who are praying for you." Then she handed him a rose. His attitude changed immediately.

After making the trip several times over the next couple of months, Diane began to search out particular people. She especially had her eye on one representative, a woman in a leadership capacity. But Diane had been warned, "She'll never talk to you."

When Diane heard that the representative's mother had just passed away, Diane went to her, handed her a red rose and said, "Representative, I'm so sorry to hear about your mother. This is for you." Diane never had any trouble gaining the ear of that representative!

Before long Diane became known as "the rose lady."

From the beginning Diane's underlying concern was, "How can we help you pass the bills that will positively affect families?"

Several state legislators in particular were extremely impressed with someone who showed a genuine interest in what they were doing and a helpful attitude. Three different ones offered her desks in their offices so that whenever she came to the state capitol, there would be a place for her to sit and work and a telephone to use.

Before long Diane started driving down to the capital every Wednesday morning. A group of legislators regularly met together on Wednesdays to pray before they went to their offices. Not only did Diane get to know which people came to pray, but she also was right there to pray along with them.

"The more you pray," Diane says, "the more you end up listening to the voice of the Lord."

Sometimes she would find herself without anyone to see or anything in particular to do. At such times she just walked through the capitol building praying.

One discouraging day when she felt she was getting absolutely nothing accomplished, she placed a call to her husband at work. "Diane," he said, "don't worry about it. Your time is in God's hands."

"One thing I learned early on," Diane says, "is to stay close to the Lord. I would never do what I am doing without first getting ready through prayer, because I never know what to expect."

In time, Diane began to have a growing influence with legislators, and sometimes they would call her in and discuss bills with her. One day a senator said to her, "Diane, you're a woman, so I hate to let you see this memo I just got and the material that came with it. But even though it's embarrassing, I feel I've got to show it to you." He handed her the envelope and abruptly left the room.

The envelope contained a bill to promote

AIDS education with some explicit examples for use in public school classrooms. The intent was obviously to teach children about homosexuality!

Diane came home distraught. She had no idea what to do, yet she was determined to do something.

"All the way home I cried, I prayed, and I cried some more," Diane says. "When I got home I went outside and dug furiously in my garden. All the time I worked, I was crying and praying, 'Lord, what can I do with this?'" She shared this information with her CWA Prayer/Action Chapter. Here was a situation that needed a massive prayer covering. And her prayer chapter agreed to hold her up in prayer.

While she wanted to let people know what was being proposed for their children, Diane felt she didn't dare send the material out through the mail. "I would have been mailing pornography!" she says.

When her husband came home, Diane showed him the proposed material; then she told him about her quandary.

"Diane," he said, "if you don't get this out to the Christian community, then you're going to be just as guilty as the ones who put it together and those who teach it. You've got a responsibility to let people know."

At her husband's suggestion, Diane went to her pastor. His advice was to go ahead and distribute the material to adult members of the church. "Yes, it's objectionable," he said, "but our people need to know." Since the material contained no pictures, it wasn't actually pornography, he assured her, and suggested she send it through the mail to others outside their church community.

"I did," Diane says, "but I couldn't bring myself to put a return address on it!"

She noticed that the information was slow in being distributed to church members. When she asked the head deacon about it, he said, "Why do you want to give that stuff out? It is horrible!"

"I know," Diane said, "but if we don't alert people, our children are going to end up reading it in their schools."

Not only was the material distributed in Diane's church, but it went also to other concerned groups throughout her state. Those efforts resulted in the end of that offensive bill!

The unique thing about Diane is that she is not really all that unique. She didn't start out politically knowledgeable. She was simply a woman who cared deeply about her family. And she believed in prayer. She prayed and sought ways to become informed. Then she could not help getting involved.

Not every one of us can be as politically involved as Diane is. But all of us can pray. And we can all ask God to show us what He would have us to do. For in God's action plan, there is a place for every single one of us, as Betsy found out.

EVERYONE WHO WANTS TO
CAN BE INVOLVED

Betsy is the mother of three little boys. When her husband left her, she was devastated. As a divorced single parent, she felt different, separated from all the "typical" Christian families around her. So she removed herself from those other families, convinced there was nothing she could do for the Lord.

When Concerned Women for America's Tenth Anniversary Conference came along, Betsy thought, *Well, I could probably host a table. No one would have to know I'm divorced or a single parent.* So she signed up to serve as a table hostess.

Not long afterward, Betsy received a copy of our newsletter listing all our conference sites. She read the list, then she read it again more closely. Her site was not listed.

Betsy called our 800 number and anxiously asked, "You aren't going to meet here in my city after all? What happened?"

"No site coordinator has come forward in your area," she was told, "so we're going to have to cancel that location."

Immediately Betsy started to pray. "Lord, I want to do something. But how can I? There's no leader here."

As clearly as if the Lord was right there beside her, Betsy told me, she heard him ask, "What about you?"

"Me!" Betsy argued. "I'm divorced! I'm a single parent!"

But once planted in her mind, the idea grew and grew. Finally, Betsy called us back and said, "Would you consider me for the site coordinator?" We told her we would.

163

Betsy applied and was accepted, and she became the area's coordinator.

After the conference was over, we got a letter from Betsy. "We had a wonderful meeting!" she wrote. Then she went on to tell us of her background in public relations and how she was able to use her skills in preparing for the conference. She told how many new members had signed up and how many prayer chapter inquiries had been received. Then she added, "But you know what was the greatest thing of all? I found that there *is* a place where God can use me."

All Betsy had asked for was a table to host. What she received was a wonderful affirmation that God had a job for her, one nobody else could fill as well.

It is the responsibility of each one of us to take the first step and pray. When we are faithful in prayer, God will show us the next step. When He does show us the particular job He has for us, it is up to us to step forward and accept it.

I would be wrong not to qualify such inspirational stories with a warning: sometimes getting involved in family issues is neither easy nor comfortable. I would suggest that anyone considering this direction should first cover the decision with prayer. You have to be willing to stand up and be counted, despite the pressure.

BE PREPARED FOR CONTROVERSY

I know the personal cost of speaking out on the issues. Testifying at the Senate Judiciary Committee hearing for Judge Robert Bork's nomination to the Supreme Court was not an easy thing to do. The entire procedure was totally foreign to me. I had no idea what to expect. All I know was that I had better go before that committee with a heart of steel, yet filled with the love of Christ.

I did have a firm foundation of prayer. All over the country, CWA women were praying for me and for the hearing. Many sent notes telling me they were behind me. As the hearings were being broadcast on national television, many prayer chapters across the United States met together to watch the live telecast so that they could be praying right then while it was all happening.

As I sat there before the Senate Judiciary Committee, I looked around at the men I was to face, men such as Senator Ted Kennedy, Senator Howard Metzenbaum, and Senator Joe Biden. Of the twelve seated on that committee, there were only two friendly faces present.

Usually in such a hearing, those who oppose the person testifying will stay around to get their licks in while the friendly ones go off to a vote on the floor or something else. But the two men who agreed with our endorsement of Judge Bork stayed in the hearing all that day.

You can believe I prayed that day! As I was being sworn in, I silently asked the Lord to still my pounding heart and to replace my nervousness with calm confidence. Then I asked Him to guide me throughout the testimony and to give me just the right words to say as one by one they began to question me. I also prayed for each of the men who would be listening. And, of course, I prayed for Judge Bork himself—for patience and endurance and wisdom.

After I finished my testimony, I sat and listened to the questions being hurled at me. Most of them had nothing at all to do with the testimony I'd just given about Judge Bork. Instead, I was asked about the membership of Concerned Women for America and the ways in which we raised money. Nobody seemed to care that we had taken the time to carefully research this fine man's background and had come up with strong, positive information about his qualification. The tactic seemed to be to try to discredit our organization and me as its representative.

Senator Metzenbaum, in his gentlemanly, yet piercing way, said, "I'm suspicious that this membership you claim is larger than the National Organization for Women, is all a figment of your imagination. I have traveled all over the state of Ohio, through our forty million people, and I have yet to meet one single member of Concerned Women for America."

Right then I determined in my heart, *Okay, Mr. Senator, I'll make sure you meet some of them in the future.*

I left that meeting knowing I could not let Senator Metzenbaum's accusations of CWA leave doubts in the minds of those people all across America who were watching the hearings on television. My first response was to the Lord. As I asked the Lord for specific wisdom regarding this false accusation, it was not long before the answer began to come through. I wrote to all of our members in Ohio and said, "Your senator says he's never seen or met you. Would you please contact him and let him know you are a member of CWA?" I included the senator's Washington address as well as his address in Ohio. I also listed his telephone numbers. CWA women had been praying. Now it was time for them to act.

And act they did! Senator Metzenbaum's phone was literally paralyzed for the next three days.

For three Ohio ladies, writing and telephoning wasn't enough. They decided to travel to Washington. When they arrived they went up to the senate office and asked to see Senator Metzenbaum. Unfortunately, he was out of his office.

As they were walking down the hall on their way out of the building, who should the ladies see walking toward them but the senator himself! With cameras hanging around their necks, looking like typical tourists, they walked right up and said, "Senator, we're from your state of Ohio and we want to meet you." Senator Metzenbaum, warm and friendly, with the political knowledge that these three ladies were potential votes, shook their hands. Then the ladies asked, "Could we have our picture taken with you?"

"Of course," the senator said.

So the women got their cameras out and posed with Senator Metzenbaum.

When the picture taking was finished, the ladies said as kindly and sincerely as possible, "Senator Metzenbaum, we want you to know we are members of

Concerned Women for America. Now you have met us, and we have the pictures to prove it!"

When Christian women become knowledgeable about issues, when they are motivated through discussion and empowered by prayer, they do indeed become a force to be reckoned with.

Knowledgeable, motivated women, we have found, are well able to communicate their convictions on paper. Congressional representatives here in Washington tell me they regularly hear from CWA women. Every time I hear from Senator Jesse Helms, for instance, he adds a note that says something such as: "I surely do appreciate your women keeping in touch with us. We want to know how they feel about specific bills." Congressman McEwen from Ohio told me one day that of all the mail he gets, the mail from CWA ladies in his district in Ohio is the most appreciated because it comes from women who are informed about the issues and have intelligent suggestions and opinions.

Education, prayer, action. Know the issues, we tell our concerned women. Know what's at stake. Then get busy and *do* something. Genuine prayer concern usually produces action.

Not too long ago, the three major television networks were threatening to advertise condoms. These ads weren't to be restricted to the off-family hours, either. They would be aired at any time of the day or night.

CWA sent out a mailing to inform our women about the networks' proposals. People who objected, we said, those who didn't want to turn on their television sets and watch a condom ad with their children, were encouraged to write to the networks and make their opinion known. We included a card. On one end was room for a note to the network. The other end could be ripped off and mailed to us for verification.

Over 628,000 notes and letters were sent— to *each* of the networks! This means over one million letters were written and mailed by concerned Americans! You can be sure the television networks listen to a response such as this.

Without a doubt there is a lot of work to be done here in the United States of America. Yet we don't want our action to stop at our borders, for there are even more desperate needs in other countries.

ACTION OUTSIDE U.S.A. BORDERS

When Jim Woodall and his team first took me up to that spot of raw jungle in Costa Rica and told me about the school he was burdened to build for Nicaraguan refugee children, it was hard to see that his dream could ever come true. There was nothing there but one tiny, ancient building tucked away in the thick jungle. Yet Jim's eyes sparkled with excitement as he pointed to one overgrown mass of jungle foliage after another and announced, "Over there is where we're going to put the school one day. The church will be here and the clinic out there."

Because we believe the future depends upon how children are educated, Concerned Women for America is committed to educating youngsters. We have prayed that God would allow us to have an influence on children through education. And there Jim was, pointing out an opportunity for us to be involved in educating little children who had been driven out of their homeland by Marxist terrorism and away from any opportunity for schooling.

"Is there any chance you need someone to share this vision with you?" I asked Jim.

My thought was that maybe in five years or so CWA could help build the school. But God saw it differently. As we began to pray about it and discuss it with others, the funds began to come in. Work teams of men volunteered from many churches to go down and help build the school.

One year later, in June of 1988, the school opened with five teachers and a principal, all of them certified Nicaraguan teachers.

Two prayers rose up from two corners of the world. In answer, God brought Jim Woodall and Concerned Women for America together and showed us we could accomplish unbelievable things when we prayed and let God lead our efforts.

On a monthly basis CWA has the privilege of providing all the expenses for the jungle school, the teachers' salaries, all the school supplies, building maintenance, uniforms and shoes for the kids, gas and maintenance for the "school boat," and noon meals for the students. Food is grown on the adjacent farm in sufficient abundance that the children are able to take some home with them. A full-time nurse is on the premises to meet the medical needs of these one hundred children.

But the most important thing of all is one hundred children and a good number of adults each year are receiving a Christian education.

Sometimes people ask me why we don't limit our efforts to needs in the United States. They insist we have enough problems right here at home without having to go outside our country looking for more.

I'm not at all apologetic about our refugee work. Those who compare the problems we have here with the problems of the destitute Nicaraguan refugees have never seen the way in which those people are forced to survive. As children of God we have an obligation to do whatever we can to help them.

I'll never forget the day Jim saw one particular little family of refugees huddled on the steps of the main cathedral in downtown San Jose, Costa Rica. Actually, they weren't an unusual sight. Since Costa Rican law required all refugees to register with the immigration department in the capital, many of these people would pour through San Jose each week.

But God wouldn't let Jim forget this one family. The smallest child, who couldn't have been more than ten months old, was trying to sleep on the bare concrete steps. He was obviously hungry, and his mother was trying to keep the hot sun off his dirty little face. Five other children sat quietly beside her, obediently waiting for their father to come back from the immigration office. When Jim came back several hours later, they were still there. He knew there was a good chance they would spend the night there, since there were very few other options for Nicaraguan refugee families. Jim stopped his car, loaded in the little family and took them home for the night to provide food and shelter for them.

Situations like this could be repeated over and over again. This was the basic reason the refugee home we call *El Reposo*—The Resting Place—was opened on April 15, 1988.

It is in San Jose, and refugees can stay there for up to three days while they register with the government for their legal status. Just the bureaucracy of going into a country that really doesn't want them is too intimidating for some to handle alone. Also, because many refugees can neither read nor write, we have made legal aid available to help them fill out their papers.

Before *El Reposo* opened, most of the people who poured across the border had nowhere but the streets to sleep. In these two years since *El Reposo* opened, more than thirty thousand people have been accommodated there.

A lady in Florida had been praying for our work with the Nicaraguans. As she prayed for them, God began to burden her heart. The need to help feed many of these hungry families became real to her. Today she sends a monthly check and each time it arrives I know she is also praying for them.

For several years we have conducted a quarterly clothing distribution in the refugee camps for these people. You cannot imagine how rotten and tattered their clothes become when they have nothing else to wear. Some arrive at the camps after walking for weeks through the jungle.

We have always tried to help them maintain

a dignity even though they were desperately needy. So in the camps we would hang the clothes on hangers and then on racks. Men, boys, girls, women, and infants all had their own sections as in a department store.

Families were brought in as one unit and allowed to select a limited supply of clothing items.

One family in particular comes to my mind. The father entered the makeshift department store with his wife and three children. They looked so pitiful, each one desperately in need of new clothes. Often in situations like this the father cannot hold his head up and look us in the eye. The humiliation of not being able to provide for his family is more than he can bear. This particular father was in such a state. After they each received their limit of clothing, he stepped up to me to speak. I looked at each of them clutching their new garments as though gifts of great value. The father said as he looked me in the eye, "Today you have reminded me that God has not forgotten about us."

You ask me is it worth all the work to help refugees? Absolutely! We can be God's hands to bless these people as we pray for them and then put action to our prayers.

We also assist many Nicaraguan refugee families on a regular basis. We've helped some start little businesses. We came across three men who were once cobblers in Nicaragua. They had all their tools with them, but they didn't have money to buy the leather goods. We supplied them with enough materials to set up a little shoemaking venture. Today three families are living on the profits from that little company.

We helped seven Nicaraguans start a small

fishing business. We supplied the fishermen with the hooks and lines, boat motors, and other odds and ends they needed. They already had the boats. They weren't looking for a handout. They just wanted a chance to make their own way.

Critics say, "What real difference are you making in the life of the average refugee down there?"

Well, one refugee leader recently told me there is hardly a Nicaraguan refugee in Costa Rica right now who hasn't been touched by Concerned Women for America. That doesn't mean we have given clothes or food to every person. What it does mean is that the tons of clothing and food, the medical care and education we have provided, have helped entire communities, approximately 300,000 people.

For the most part these refugees are hard working people. They know what it's like to put in a full day's work. But through circumstances beyond their control, they suddenly had to flee their country and leave all their earthly possessions behind. Now they find themselves in a situation where the fathers can no longer provide for their children, a situation that destroys family life. Dignity and self-respect is gone. His wife is dressed in rags; his children are hungry and swollen with parasites. And the father, whose responsibility it is to provide for his family, finds himself helpless and humiliated. The Costa Rican government will not permit them to hold down jobs in Costa Rican businesses because it destroys the work opportunities for their own citizens.

The refugees are in a situation where there

is nothing they can do to help themselves. But there's plenty we can do. Some of our CWA members have collected clothes. Some have given money. Hundreds have donated their time to go down and help with the distribution. Doctors have worked on medical teams. Teams of men from local churches have taken vacation time to help us. And many, many have prayed faithfully.

For far too long Christians—especially Christian women—have remained removed from issues and politics and from taking action.

Diane was not able to get really involved until she found out what was at stake. Betsy didn't discover there was a niche no one could fill as well as she until she stepped forward and made herself available. The lady in Florida didn't know she could provide food to desperate Nicaraguans until she became involved through prayer and then asked what more she could do.

We want women to *know* so that they can pray. And after they have prayed, we want them to *act*. That's God's way.

CHAPTER
9

THE POWER TO MOVE IN GOD'S STRENGTH

"When I told a friend about how God's encouragement came just when I needed it most, she said, 'He's never too early and He's never too late. He's always right on time,'" a CWA member from California wrote.

We look at circumstances and we despair. Things appear to go wrong. On all sides evil seems to triumph. In frustration and hopelessness we cry out, "Where are You, God?"

From our perspective, we are only winners when everything goes our way and we come out on top. We want to see the opposition lying at our feet. In the previous chapter, I admitted that standing up for family issues is not easy. But it is possible, because God gives us armor that protects us as we move forward in His strength, even when we seem to be losing the battle. Let's look at this armor with which God equips us:

THE ARMOR OF GOD

1. *The Wisdom to See the Battle from God's Perspective*

God's perspective is so much broader. He alone sees the whole picture. How, then, can we really judge the wins or the losses? The answer is simple: we can't by using man's limited wisdom. We are victorious, however, because God has a different vantage point.

Let me tell you about Betty Batey.

Betty met Frank Batey at a church retreat. After a short courtship, they were married. But Betty's happiness didn't last long. Shortly before the birth of their child Betty made a horrifying discovery: her husband was homosexual. Frank admitted his secret life to Betty, and shortly thereafter the two were separated.

Frank's and Betty's son, Brian, was born in 1972. Three years later, when her divorce became final, Betty was awarded custody of the child. Frank was given visitation rights.

From the beginning, father and son had a close relationship. So Betty was crushed when, at the age of ten, Brian came home in tears after a visit with his father. At first the boy refused to tell his mother what had upset him so terribly. But finally he blurted it out: Brian had seen his father in bed, engaged in a sexual act with another man.

"I don't want to go back!" Brian insisted. "Not ever again!"

Betty was both horrified and alarmed. Under the circumstances she wasn't about to force her son to go back to his father's house.

Frank saw it differently, and he took Betty to court.

Betty told the judge that her son didn't want to be with his father, and she explained the reason why. Frank argued that Betty was purposely preventing

Brian from visiting him. The dispute—and the court appearances—went on and on.

Totally exasperated and seemingly prejudiced against Betty, the judge awarded custody of Brian to Frank and gave Betty visitation rights.

The next thing Brian knew, he was being whisked off to Palm Springs to live with his father and his father's live-in sodomite partner. Betty wasn't even allowed to tell him goodbye.

At least once a day the boy telephoned his mother. In tears, he poured out his misery. One day he threatened, "I'm going to run away!"

Betty pleaded with Brian to do his best to stick it out for ten days. "Then you can come home for a visit," she promised.

Betty's heart broke for her son. Yet, since she couldn't afford to pay her attorney's fees for the last trial, how could she possibly consider going to court again? By the time Brian arrived home for his visit, Betty was frantic. In desperation she packed their belongings and took the boy out of the state. It was the only way Betty felt she could protect Brian from the perverted influence of Frank and his homosexual friends.

For a year and a half, mother and son remained in hiding, moving between Texas, Oklahoma, and Colorado to avoid detection. Moments of peace and joy were hard to come by.

"For seventeen months God allowed us to live in a beautiful place where we took care of a little lady," Betty says. This time was very valuable in Brian's life. The closeness to his mother gave her a chance to teach Christian principles as she home-schooled him rather than send him out in public. "Then late one night I got a telephone call warning me to leave town. 'The FBI is looking for you because kidnap charges have been filed against you,' the caller said. 'You've got to go right away, by ten o'clock for sure.' That meant Brian and I only had a few hours."

Betty had not seen her parents or her family in a year-and-a-half. "We have an extremely close family," she says. "There were times I thought I just couldn't make it through another day not being able to talk to them. I felt so very isolated."

Betty's family dared not visit her, for that would mean running the risk of exposing her hiding place. Even the rare telephone calls had to be placed carefully and with the help of a trusted go-between. Yet for a reason her family could never explain, they suddenly felt compelled to fly to see her. The timing was such that they were with her when she got the call.

"If they hadn't been there, I don't know what I would have done," Betty says. "But God knew my pain. And He knew how badly I needed my family. Brian and I were able to talk to them and hug them before we started running again."

After a year of battling the courts, Frank managed to get kidnapping charges filed against Betty. When Betty discovered there was a warrant out for her arrest, she went to her pastor and told him her situation. At his urging she agreed to turn herself in—herself, but not Brian. Someone associated with the church took in the boy. Betty wasn't even told where he was. That way, when she was asked about his whereabouts, she could truthfully say, "I don't know."

Betty and her pastor assumed she would be granted a new custody hearing in Colorado and that this time it would be fair, and the court would give due consideration of Brian's objections to living with his father. Instead, Betty was immediately taken into custody by federal authorities and locked up in jail.

When day after day after day went by and Betty still was not released, Brian became convinced that the judge wasn't going to let his mother out until Brian was handed over to the court. So without anyone's knowledge the boy, now thirteen, turned himself in. Immediately he was returned to California. Soon after, Betty, too, was sent to California—for trial.

Ordinarily, in a case such as this, a child would immediately be placed with the custodial parent. For Brian that would have meant going to live with his father. Our CWA attorney persuaded the court to put the boy in a neutral setting—a foster home. Then, because she had voluntarily turned herself in, Betty was immediately released from custody.

Right away Betty saw two distinct answers to prayer—Brian wouldn't be sent to his father and she wouldn't have to wait in jail for the trial.

But there were also frustrating battle losses. To the particular judge assigned to this case, the fact that Frank was homosexual and living with a homosexual partner was totally irrelevant. She would never let it be discussed in court even after the initial evidence had been presented. Every time our attorneys tried to bring the subject up, they were immediately cut off.

"That judge was determined to see my son taken away from me," Betty says.

Others also seemed determined. One surprising supporter of Frank was a respected member of the local Christian community, a man who worked with young people. He wrote a character letter in favor of Frank and his sodomy partner, Craig, encouraging the judge to place Brian in their home. Admitting it was an unusual request since the men were homosexual, the man insisted the two—his friends—were of good character.

In the end, before he died of AIDS, the letter writer was depicted in one newspaper as a hero. Another—a gay newspaper—carried a picture of his homosexual partner.

Even Brian's court-appointed attorney—the person whose responsibility it was to help Brian—fought against allowing the boy to go home to his mother. Brian's own attorney! The only reason ever given was that Betty was rigid. She insisted that her son live by rules. No evidence was ever presented that Betty was an unfit mother.

"As our case became publicized, people wrote to encourage me," Betty says. "Many sent me Scripture. Several reminded me that 'Weeping may endure in the night, but joy comes in the morning.' How I clung to that verse!"

184

At first, the criminal case against Betty was thrown out. But the state of California appealed that decision, and the appeals court reinstated the criminal charges. That decision was appealed all the way to the United States Supreme Court, which declined to review it. Betty would have to stand trial yet again.

After having been in court close to one hundred times already, Betty was worn out. Attorney Michael Farris told her, "They have a plea bargain to offer you. If you will enter a plea of guilty, they will reduce the charges from a felony to a misdemeanor with no jail time and a minimum fine. The decision is yours."

"I'm so weary," Betty told Michael. "I've fought so many battles all these years. I've done my best. Maybe I should just go ahead and say I'm guilty." Then she said, "Just let me pray about it, Michael. I'll ask God to show me what I should do. Maybe this is the way it should end."

As she knelt before Him in prayer, the Lord brought to Betty's mind the sparrows Jesus referred to in Matthew. They are so important to God that not one of them falls to the ground apart from His will. And the "lilies of the field, . . . they neither toil nor spin; yet . . . even Solomon in all his glory was not arrayed like one of these" (Matt. 6:28–29). And us, God's children? Why, the very hairs of your head are numbered. That's how personal a God we serve.

"It was almost as if God spoke out loud to me that day. 'Try me,' He seemed to say. 'Prove Me.'"

Betty had her answer. She called Michael

Farris and Cimron Campbell and told them, "We're going to court. I don't know what's going to happen, but we're going to court."

A jury was called and everything was readied. However, the judge made his decision without submitting the case to the jury. The judge said, "After considering the evidence, I can see the reason for this mother's fears. I find the defendant, Betty Batey, not guilty of kidnapping." The court found that Betty had no criminal intent in removing her son.

When Brian was about fifteen years old and still living in a foster home, he got into trouble. This was no real surprise; an expert witness had predicted it would happen if the judge continued to keep Brian away from his mother. The trouble was so minor that normally nothing would have come of it—except that the same judge trying Betty's case also had authority to preside over juvenile cases. Brian had repeatedly told the judge that he would not stay with his father and would run away. She, the judge, would now have power over Brian to force him to stay with Frank.

The judge asked that Brian's case be assigned to her, then she put him and the other three boys involved on probation. Within a year, she dismissed the other three boys, but she kept Brian on probation for no valid reason. Then, without notifying anyone else, the judge called Brian in and offered him a horrible choice. Brian reported to Betty that the judge gave him a choice between either living with his father or she would put him in the juvenile detention hall. He had to make the decision.

Brian called his mother and said, "I don't want to go live with him, Mom, but I don't want to be locked up, either. So I'm going to tell the judge I'll move in with Frank."

All around the country, a host of people committed themselves to join Betty in prayer. They prayed privately, they prayed in twos and threes, they prayed in groups, they prayed in churches. All across the nation people brought Betty Batey and her son before the Lord. Strangers called our CWA office just to tell us they were praying for Betty and her son.

In our CWA prayer groups, Betty Batey became a household word. The hearts of women everywhere were wrenched at the thought of a godly mother actually losing her son to a homosexual father. They found it unbelievable that a judge in the United States of America could actually think it preferable for a teenage boy to be tossed into such a situation than to be allowed to live with his Christian mother.

In his Palm Springs home, Frank took Brian to a psychologist who urged the boy to love Frank and to accept his homosexuality. Then he and Craig did what shrewd adults who are trying to win a teenager's heart often do—they gave him unsupervised freedom. That's not all. They also bought him a membership in a teenage nightclub and encouraged him to attend all-night rock concerts. They bought him all kinds of clothes and almost anything else he wanted. Frank and

Craig lived in a big house with a swimming pool, and Brian could use it whenever he wanted.

It wasn't long before Brian began to see that life with Dad could be fun.

Never much of a student, Brian didn't do well in the public school in which his father enrolled him. The boy quit going to classes and his father didn't even know it for more than a month. Brian spent his days getting into mischief with other boys.

Frank provided a horrible environment for Brian, yet the probation officer in charge did nothing. Brian was not receiving proper parental supervision nor proper probationary supervision.

Betty's attorney noted that Frank, who was gaunt and had a hacking cough, didn't look at all healthy. Suspecting something was wrong, he asked the court to require that Frank be examined for AIDS. Although the judge is supposed to look at the health, safety, and welfare of the minors in her charge, she refused to require Frank and Craig to be tested for the disease.

A year later, Frank died in Brian's arms, a victim of AIDS.

Grief-stricken for his father, with whom he had now lived for almost two years, Brian was determined to be around to make arrangements for the funeral. He refused to leave the Palm Springs home.

Under the law, if one parent dies, custody automatically goes to the other parent. A hearing isn't even held. But for seventeen-year-old Brian, things were different. Without a hearing, the same judge who forced Brian to live with Frank appointed Craig, Frank's homosexual partner, as Brian's temporary guardian. Never before had such a ruling been made in the United States of America.

"I believe the good Lord has our tears bottled up in heaven," Betty says. "Well, He sure has barrels of mine!"

Yet through it all Betty's faith remained strong—although she admits there were times she surely didn't feel it. "To look at me and the way I reacted, you'd have thought I didn't think anything good was ever going to come of it all. But deep down in my mind and soul, I trusted God."

For close to four months, our CWA attorney tried to get a new hearing. He also tried to get the presiding judge disqualified as not being impartial. She refused to be moved.

The judge ordered that Brian's permanent custody be awarded to Craig—never mind that the man's only connection with the boy was that he was Brian's father's former sex partner. Even the attorney's request that Craig be tested for AIDS was refused.

Attorney Cimron Campbell was outraged. "I've never before heard of such a ruling!" he said. "Where is the logic in taking a minor away from his parent and placing him with someone who is likely dying from a horrible disease—a deadly disease with many unknown risks?"

The judge ruled that the home of the homosexual partner was a more "stable and wholesome environment" for Brian than the home of his mother. To return Brian to the home of his born-again Christian mother, ruled the judge, would be "detrimental to said minor." No substantive evidence was ever introduced to show that Betty's home was in any way unwholesome.

Things couldn't have looked more bleak. Yet Betty never stopped saying, "God is in charge. I know He's going to bring Brian through this. All we have to do is to keep on praying."

As events turned more discouraging, some people, assuming it was all over, quit praying for Betty and Brian. Not Betty. She refused to give up.

"A lot of things happened I didn't want to see happen," Betty says, "but I was still a winner."

Many people would look at Betty Batey and shake their heads in disbelief. How could she possibly consider herself a winner in the face of such obvious failures? How could she insist God was going to work everything out when everything was going so badly?

When we pray and pray and pray yet see no answer, it's terribly hard to keep from getting discouraged. I know. I've been there.

"When that happens," says Evelyn Smith, the widow who refused to rent to unmarried couples, "all we can do is watch for the Lord's way and wait for the Lord's time. My case has lost—supposedly. But it isn't over yet. And no case is really lost until the end."

Along the way, simply by virtue of having endured, every one of us who had to go through a difficult time can be an encouragement to others.

CHAPTER 10

A CHALLENGE THAT COULD CHANGE OUR WORLD

"Dear Beverly," wrote a woman from Farmington, Arkansas, "I am outraged at the burning of our American flag. My husband is a twice wounded World War II veteran living on a 10 percent disability pension and social security. He says as he lay wounded in a foxhole waiting for a medic for two days and nights, he was never as happy as he was at the sight of the American flag telling him they had come to help him. The flag is our symbol of peace, help, and hope."

A woman wrote from Hawaii: "As the wife of a dedicated naval officer, I am very aware of the dangers many of our military people face every day. My husband is now patrolling the ocean (who knows where?) in a submarine—probably very close to enemy territory. Although he doesn't face direct combat, he is still putting his life on the line for the United States of America. The work of CWA gives me the opportunities to ensure that our country is worth the sacrifices we make as a military family."

People say Christians—especially Christian

women—don't want to get involved. How wrong those people are!

In Matthew 5:13–14, God commands us to be the salt of the earth and the light of the world. If enough Christians take on the true nature of salt and work to preserve what America has traditionally stood for, then we will cause people to thirst for Christ. If we allow our light to shine brightly enough and if we hold it high enough, people will begin to see our country in the brilliance of God's truths.

If we combine the qualities of salt and light, America will indeed be a source of God's richest blessings for our children, our children's children and the entire world.

Many women say, "But the job is so big, and I am so limited. What can I possibly do that will make a difference?"

I'm glad you asked!

All over the country ordinary, everyday people—people not much different from you—*are* doing things, and they *are* making a difference.

YOU CAN PRAY WITH YOUR FAMILY

Are we too busy to include our children in our prayer time? Do we take the time to build a hunger for communicating with the Lord through prayer in the hearts of our children?

One lovely family comes to my mind. Tim and I were ministering in Oklahoma several years ago. We stayed in the guest room of this special family who had two sons.

This father, John, was a wonderful God-fearing man who desired to build strong Christian principles into his children. His sons, ages ten and sixteen, were outstanding young men. John had a great gift for encouraging people to pray, including his own children.

That evening when the service was over, this couple decided to take us out for a snack before returning back to their home. The sons had stayed home to do their studies. As we drove along, the father's car phone rang and it was the oldest boy calling.

"Dad," he said, "how late are you going to be?" The father answered that we would be home shortly. The boy continued, "Well, I know you always pray with us before we go to sleep and I wondered if you wanted me to wait up or will you wake me up when you get home?"

The father warmly told the boy he could wait up for him. But then the younger boy took the phone and asked, "Dad what about me?" The dad said, "Son, you had better go on to bed, but I will pray with you now."

As we continued to drive through town, the father cradled the phone against his shoulder and prayed a prayer of love, guidance and concern to the Lord for his child. It was a beautiful conversation with the Lord about his young son. No wonder the boys did not want to go to bed without this tender touch from their earthly and heavenly Fathers.

This father shared with us that wherever he is, even when he is travelling and has to call home, he tries to pray with his sons every night. For them, it would be like going without a meal to miss their nightly prayers. An appetite for prayer has been created in their young hearts.

YOU CAN COMMIT CONCERNS TO PRAYER

With so much to be done, with so many challenges and attacks on our families, we must never stop praying. If Elijah had sent his servant six times to look at the sky and he had come back that sixth time to report, "There is no cloud in the sky," and Elijah had said, "Enough is enough" and dropped the matter, the prophet would never have seen God's miracle.

Don't quit praying. You may be right on the verge of an answer.

The majority of us are steadfastly opposed to abortion. But how many of us have really prayed strenuously over the millions of babies who have been killed and over what is happening to America because of this slaughter? It is the strenuous praying that reaches the heart of God.

God impressed on Paulette Brack from South Texas the need to pray about two particular issues: abortion and school prayer. And she has committed herself to pray regularly about these two issues.

"I think we overlook the power of prayer because of its simplicity," Paulette says. "If Christians are supposed to be salt and light, they had better *be* salt and light!"

And what about our families? Do we settle for prayer clichés, or do we really lay them before God?

"There's so little I can do to protect my little girl," says a woman from South Carolina. "I'm not at school with her when she's learning all this stuff. So every morning before she gets out of the car and goes into the school, we pray together. I say, 'Lord, protect her from the bad things and let her learn the good things.' And then all day, whenever she comes into my mind, I whisper another prayer for her."

If anything can get to the heart of a mother, it's her children. We so desperately desire that they stay on the right path and not wander off. I know. I've been there. And like Elijah I've just had to keep going back again and again and again.

God doesn't always answer our prayer overnight. Often it's a slow process of watching a loved one turning back a little at a time. Yet how wonderful it is to see even the tiny signs that an older son or daughter is coming back to the Lord, something as small as taking you to lunch and saying, "I'll pray today."

From California came this letter: "I have been praying for those fathers jailed in Nebraska, and I have decided to take some action. Enclosed is my gift. I would send more but this is all I have. I am ten years old."

And from fourteen-year-old Jeni in Arizona: "Today my mother received your letter about Planned Parenthood. After she had read the material, she let me read it. I was shocked and appalled by what I saw!"

Jeni added this P.S.: "I will be drafting a letter to the two congressmen mentioned in your letter tomorrow. I know that I'm still very young, but if there is *anything* that I can do to help you out, please let me know right away. My prayers are with you."

See how prayer leads to action? A woman

in New York wrote: My prayer chain started a ministry in a women's prison where women were serving long-term sentences. As first all we could do was send packages of writing papers, pens, and socks to the women who were entering the prison (about forty per month). We prayed over the packages, dropped them off, and were never able to meet the women.

After a year of this, we won the heart of the warden, and we are now meeting the women. Prayer chains have been started in the prison now!

At Concerned Women for America's Tenth Anniversary Celebration, Dr. James Dobson said,

"I don't think I can stand the thought of my grandchildren growing up in a world that has no recollection and no memory of the things that I'd give my life for.

"I still believe we can awaken that vast army, of women especially, who typically care enough about their families to do something about it. The hope is in prayer, Beverly, and I know you know that. It is not in might and power. It's getting on our faces before God and asking Him to heal our land."

Yes, friends, prayer does work! But we need to work at praying.

YOUR ACTIONS CAN BE AN EXAMPLE
FOR YOUR CHILDREN

A young mother from New Hampshire, who describes herself as "just an everyday, insignificant lady," sent me a note. She wrote about how impressionable children are. When she began working with the CWA, she said, she had no idea how her daughters would be affected.

When she went to her prayer chapter meetings, her little girls—ages six, four, and two—went along. She also took them when she went to pray outside abortion clinics.

One day she caught sight of her little girls playing over in a corner of their family room. The six year old was holding a CWA meeting for her sisters. They were praying for America. The child had seen her mother hand out some of our flyers, so she made some flyers of her own, one of which her mother sent to me. On the outside it said: "CWA—We love children." Inside there were stick-figure children. "Mothers take care of their children," it said. On the back was printed; "We pray for one another."

"I never realized it," the mom wrote, "but while I was trying to make a change in my neighborhood, I was also influencing the lives of my own children.

"Since God ordained government, we as Christians should do everything we can to bring about the kind of government that would honor our Lord. And in doing so, that would give us a good environment for our children to grow up in," says Elizabeth Roessger of Wisconsin.

"My main concern at this time is my three grandchildren," says Jimmie Nell Ecker of Colorado, mother of three and grandmother of three. "All my life I thought, I'm going to fight the law of averages. I will make a difference. I want my grandchildren to feel the same way. I'll do something as long as I live. Even if the world is not still the same, I want my grandchildren to say, 'My grandmother always tried to make the world a better place.'"

YOU CAN BE AN ENCOURAGEMENT TO OTHERS

"When I'd be feeling really low," said Ken Roberts, the teacher who read the Bible in his classroom, "a letter of support would come, or sometimes even a phone call. Today was a really heavy-duty day, but I got two letters from people who were praying for me. Their timing was really good."

Some people make an effort to do or say just the right thing at just the right time. Others seem to do the opposite.

When Jolene Cox decided to proceed with her equal access suit against the library in Oxford, Mississippi, a woman in her prayer chapter told her, "But, Jolene, what about your social position in the community? It's going to be ruined!"

Jolene answered, "My social position means nothing to me. My position in the Lord's kingdom means everything."

We need to be sure we are working for God as an encouragement, not against Him.

What a ministry encouragement is! After the earthquake in Coalinga, California, we received a letter from the prayer chapter there thanking us for our prayers and concern. A billboard outside their town reads: "Jesus is Lord of Coalinga." Many of the residents were convinced that was true. Their little town was flattened, yet there wasn't a single fatality!

YOU CAN USE YOUR TALENTS AND ABILITIES

Three days a week, Carole Wells travels from Spartanburg, South Carolina, to Columbia to represent the citizens of her community in the State House of Representatives. Carole is "an ordinary women who decided she could help change the world by believing in an extraordinary God and answering His call to run for state office."

In the primary election, Carole beat the incumbent three to one. "He campaigned against me as 'the housewife,'" she says. "All the other housewives voted for me!"

Carole Wells has what it takes to be an effective politician. But she doesn't agree that it's just a job for the few. "Everyone needs to be involved in politics," she insists. "If you're not running for office, help someone who is."

Evie, a mother of three boys from Santa Barbara, California, isn't a politician. But she surely can make signs and posters. She uses them for right-to-life demonstrations.

"I think it's important to have signs and posters that are tasteful, attractive, and professional looking," Evie says.

What talents, abilities, or interests do you

have? Whatever they are, you can use them to make a difference.

YOU CAN MAKE A DIFFERENCE
RIGHT WHERE YOU ARE

Yes, one women can make a difference—wherever she is. In Wisconsin. In Maryland. In Pennsylvania.

Just one woman in Wisconsin.

A lady by the name of Linda wrote to tell me about an experience she had in her hometown of Jackson, Wisconsin.

At the end of the checkout counters in a local store, Linda said, are a few video games. The purpose of the games is to entertain children while their parents check out. When she heard a blood-curdling scream, Linda's attention focused on one particular game.

"It was a game called 'The Golden Axe,'" Linda explained. "The object was to mutilate your opponent by chopping off his limbs."

Linda was appalled! She wrote a letter to the store headquarters and told them she found the game repulsive and in terribly bad taste. She was sure, she told those in charge, that they wanted to be a family store. But if so, encouraging such brutal behavior as fun was inexcusable.

"I asked them to remove the game," Linda

wrote, "and told them they would hear from me until they did."

A week later Linda's husband returned from the store. With a big smile, he reported there was an empty hole where "The Golden Axe" had once stood.

"Ten days after I sent my letter," Linda said, "I received a gracious letter of apology from the store. They thanked me for letting them know the game was there." Then she added, "This situation taught me that one woman *can* and *does* make a difference right in her own hometown."

We all have a responsibility to be aware of what is going on around us and then to respond to it. I could never know what is happening in the stores in Jackson, Wisconsin, because I never shop there. But Linda knew. And she did something about it.

In Central California, CWA members made themselves available on election day. A local television channel periodically showed the name of Concerned Women for America on the screen along with a telephone number that people could call if they needed help getting to the polls to vote. As the calls came in, volunteers went to the caller's home and drove them to the polls.

Just one woman in Maryland.

When Geri, a Maryland mom, looked over a copy of the Christmas choral program her young son brought home from school, she was puzzled by the songs listed. One she found offensive. Upon closer inspection, she was surprised that of thirteen songs to be presented five were Jewish, and the rest were secular. Not one spiritual or Christian song appeared on the program. Concerned by what seemed to be purposeful exclusion, she called the superintendent.

"The teacher chooses the songs," he told Geri. "But we do expect 'balance.'" He encouraged Geri to pursue the matter with the teacher.

Geri did so, and the teacher happily eliminated the offensive song and included two with a Christian flavor. "I didn't know I could use them," the teacher explained.

Just one woman in Pennsylvania.

In Lancaster, Pennsylvania, Pam reported that organized parental opposition kept a sex clinic from opening near a local junior high school. Parents of students at the public school thoughtfully and intelligently expressed their opposition to the proposed clinic, and the school board responded by scrapping the clinic plans.

What's happening in your community? Keep your eyes open. When you see a problem, don't just complain—do something. Pray for direction. Like Linda and Geri and Pam, you can make a difference when you ask for wisdom and guidance. In California. Or South Dakota. Or Alaska. In any one of our fifty states.

It's amazing what can happen when prayer is a conversation between you and God, not a one-way dialogue. All across this country men, women, and young people have prayed about a problem and have been led to take action to right the wrong.

Cindy Johnson, from Atlanta, Georgia, went to Costa Rica with me in 1989 to help with the clothing distribution for the Nicaraguan refugees.

"It was heartbreaking to see young boys living without any families in these camps," she wrote in a letter home. "They would stand in the tropical heat all day to get a pair of used pants and a cotton shirt."

To another she wrote, "It's not just a set of clothing we give, but encouragement, dignity, and the hope that people in America do care about them."

Cindy had an opportunity to show her concern in a tangible way, and she grabbed it.

When we are open to the Lord's leading, He will lead us. There is no question about it.

THE MIGHTIEST WEAPON OF ALL—PRAYER

The 1990s is not the first time America has been on the brink of moral devastation and spiritual bankruptcy. In fact, each time our nation approached the turn of a century in her brief history, there have been conditions that were so severe that only the power of prayer could resolve.

In the late 1790s the circumstances in this young nation had reached their worst conditions. A very concerned Baptist minister, Isaac Backus, had a special touch from the Holy Spirit which left him with a new zeal for prayer and exhortation. He said, "There's only one power on earth that commands the power of heaven—prayer."

Because of his deepened experience with God through prayer he wrote a *Plea for Prayer for Revival of Religion* and mailed it to ministers of every denomination in our country. This was a plea for pastors to set aside the first Monday of each month to open their churches all day and conduct extraordinary prayer for revival.

First the Methodists, then Baptists, Presbyterians, Congregationalists, Reformed and the Moravians agreed to join together in this network of organized prayer meetings.

The Holy Spirit began a real outpouring in these churches that spread across the frontier and produced such men as Charles Finney and Peter Cartwright. This sweeping revival across the nation returned the helm of the country back to the godly.

This spiritual renewal began to diminish in the mid-1800s. The effects of this transformation eroded, and judgement came in the form of a terrible economic and social crash. Thousands of merchants were out of business as banks failed and railroads went into bankruptcy. Unemployment skyrocketed. New York City alone had over 30,000 men without work.

The American people had come through several years of making plenty of money, and as they got richer they turned their backs on God. The spiritual conditions had once again deteriorated.

In 1857 a businessman named Jeremiah

Lanphier in New York City became so burdened by the moral decay and spiritual coldness that he started a weekly noon-day prayer meeting at the Dutch Church in downtown New York. He announced the meetings by handing out ads.

On the first day he arrived for the prayer meeting he found he was all alone. After waiting for twenty-five minutes six men came in. They prayed together and agreed to come back next week. The following week there were fourteen and each week thereafter the number grew. Shortly after, they decided to meet at noon everyday. As their number continued to grow, they filled the Dutch Reformed Church, the Methodist Church and every public building in downtown New York. It was reported that within six months, over 10,000 businessmen were meeting to pray for their salvation, to confess their sin, and to pray for revival.

The movement began to spread throughout New England. It then crossed the Atlantic to Ireland, Scotland, Wales, England, South Africa and South India.

The effect of this revival lasted over 40 years and it all began with one man burdened to pray. It has been reported that more than one million were saved during this prayer movement. And countless ministries began during this period. Such ministries as D. L. Moody, Ira Sankey and the founding of the Salvation Army under the direction of William and Catherine Booth all had their beginning during this spiritual awakening.

But once again, at the turn of the 20th century, there was a great need for a spiritual renewal because Christians were growing spiritually cold and indifferent. Special prayer meetings were being held at many of the Bible centers of America, such as Moody Bible Institute in Chicago and Keswick Convention in New England. People were praying in other lands as well, such as Korea and India—praying that God would send another spiritual awakening in this turn of the century. The Lord shook this nation in 1905 with transforming conviction because people were praying everywhere. Churches were filled, overflowing with prayer meetings. The mayor of Denver called for a day of prayer; by 10 A.M. churches were filled: before noon the stores began to close, including schools and the state legislature; and it is reported that 12,000 attended prayer meetings in downtown theaters and halls. Twenty-five percent of the Yale University student body were enrolled in Bible studies and prayer meetings. The impact was tremendous. As prayer continued to spread, thousands of people had their lives straightened out and received forgiveness of sins. Judges had little to do since they had no cases to try. Rapes, robberies, murder, burglaries, embezzlements all had come to a halt. There was great unemployment among police officers because they were hardly needed. America had been touched by the Holy Spirit again!

It is now approaching the coming of the next turn of the century, the year 2000, and our nation once again needs a spiritual awakening. The moral decay and spiritual coldness is at its worst condition again. The children of our nation are becoming the innocent victims of America's depravity and deceit.

Who will be the one to start the prayer movement this time that could begin the spiritual awakening we need so desperately? Could it be you? Or maybe your pastor? Will it be a small group of ladies in a CWA prayer chapter? CWA ladies who are not seeking fame but instead gravely concerned over the condition of our country?

It was Robert E. Lee who said, "Knowing that intercessory prayer is our mightiest weapon and the supreme call for all Christians today, I pleadingly urge our people everywhere to pray. Believing that prayer is the greatest contribution that our people can make in this critical hour, I humbly urge that we take time to pray—to really pray. Let there be prayer at sunup, at noonday, at sundown, and midnight—all through the day. Let us pray for our children, our youth, our aged, our pastors, our homes. Let us pray for our churches. Let us pray for ourselves, that we may not lose the word 'concern' out of our Christian vocabulary. Let us pray for those who have never known Jesus Christ and redeeming love, for moral forces everywhere, for our national leaders. Let prayer be our passion. Let prayer be our practice."

We are concerned as Robert E. Lee has stated. We are the concerned men and women of America.

Our goal is to have over 10,000 prayer chapters praying earnestly by the turn of the century. We need to have prayer chapters in our churches, our homes and every community. Remember 2 Chronicles 7:14, "If My people who are called by My name will humble themselves, and pray and seek My face, and turn from their wicked ways, then I will hear from heaven, and will forgive their sin and heal their land."

Will you pray with us for that to happen?

Pray expectantly!

APPENDIX

QUESTIONS AND ANSWERS ABOUT CWA

What is a prayer/action chapter?

A prayer/action chapter is a group of women (and men) committed to protecting the rights of the family through prayer and action. CWA seeks to have a prayer chapter in every church and community across the United States.

A chapter is part of our *national* prayer/action network. The chapters will be part of a nation-wide effort to pray and act as an organized team on specific concerns.

CWA provides an atmosphere in which women can develop leadership skills. They can also learn how to effectively and positively communicate their concerns about family-related issues to influence their community.

How often do prayer chapters meet?

Prayer chapters are encouraged to meet at least once a month to become informed on issues in their community, state and nation, to pray specifically and take appropriate action.

Is CWA a church organization?

CWA leaders do agree to a basic statement of beliefs, but we are not controlled by a religious organization or denomination. We are comprised of people from various denominations. In some cases, pastors have chosen to promote the prayer chapter meeting in their church as an officially recognized ministry within that church. For this reason, CWA prefers that chapters be organized church-by-church so that the chapter members feel at liberty in their own church setting to pray and act in unity rather than engage in possible doctrinal differences.

Is CWA a political organization?

No. CWA is a nonprofit, educational organization that seeks to keep people informed of issues affecting the God-ordained institution of the family. CWA is not a political committee by law.

Does CWA have a structure of accountability?

Yes. CWA has a structure of accountability from the chapter leader to local leadership and finally to the national office in Washington, D.C. The CWA President and staff are held accountable for their actions to CWA's national board of directors.

How do I become a prayer/action chapter leader?

CWA invites interested people to request an

Application for Leadership by contacting the Area Representative in their state or by writing to

Concerned Women for America
Office of Field Development
370 L'Enfant Promenade, S.W., Suite 800
Washington, D.C. 20024

You must be a current member of CWA to serve in leadership. You may join CWA by enclosing a donation with your application. Your donation enables you to receive the monthly CWA national newsletter, so that you may stay informed on current issues and prayer concerns.

Following approval of your application, CWA will provide you with information about getting your chapter started and provide you the name of our local representative to give you further guidance.

CWA looks forward to seeing the army of prayer chapters that will emerge in this decade!

The effectual, fervent prayer of a righteous man availeth much (see also, 2 Chron. 7:14, 1 Tim. 2:1–2).

HISTORY OF CWA

A small group of women in Southern California became concerned that the women in their churches seemed to know so little about the growing influence of the women's liberation movement, the effects of the International Women's Year (IWY) in 1977, and the hidden agenda of the proposed Equal Rights Amendment. As they shared their concerns with friends, it became apparent that there was a general interest in doing something, but no one seemed to know how to begin.

Beverly LaHaye called the group together for prayer and discussion. Several members of the group were involved in speaking at numerous neighborhood gatherings to expose the evils of the IWY's agenda and the ERA. It soon became impossible to meet all the demands for speaking and information on these subjects, so a meeting was set for a Monday evening in October, 1978, at a public auditorium. Interested friends from local churches and the community in San Diego County were invited to a pro-America rally to learn the truth behind the feminist agenda—once and for all, we thought.

However, it was evident that many had a keen interest in this matter, not only for information but also for action. Many of the approximately 1200 who attended wanted more—more information and more involvement. In January, 1979, nine women met for the first board meeting to officially launch the organization of Concerned Women for America. Not one of them at that time foresaw an organization that would someday have national recognition and influence.

A simple newsletter was sent out to give progress reports on the ERA and any other activities of CWA. Information spread from one state to another, and again it became evident that a few women in Southern California could not carry the load without more help.

"Chapters" were formed in the places where a concerned woman was willing to lead her church or community friends. As numerous chapters grew in a state, a coordinator was needed; thus, the CWA Area Representatives came into being.

The Prayer/Action Chapters are at the very heart of CWA and are largely responsible for CWA's rapid growth and effectiveness in grassroots efforts and influence. Every Chapter Leader has a unique responsibility and opportunity to make a difference in her community, state, and nation.

God bless you as you begin this venture! Do it as unto the Lord!

CWA CONCERNS

• We are concerned about the personal dignity of the individual and the increasing deprivation of freedom and human rights.
• We are concerned about the impact changing roles of men and women are having on families in our society and the attempt to eliminate the natural distinctions between men and women through legislation such as the Equal Rights Amendment.
• We are concerned about the rights of the unborn.
• We are concerned about the declining quality of education in public schools and the increasing emphasis on secular humanism in classrooms and textbooks.
• We are concerned about the potential loss of religious freedom due to increased governmental intervention.
• We are concerned about the security of our nation and

the increasing pressure to weaken the country's defenses.

• We are concerned about the fiscal responsibility of the government and its impact on our nation.

• We are concerned about sexual promiscuity, especially among young people and society's ineffective response to it.

• We are concerned about the increasing availability of pornography and the lack of judicial enforcement of existing laws.

• We are concerned about the growing acceptance of homosexuality and other "alternative" lifestyles and their destructive impact on society.

• We are concerned about the morally deteriorating condition of the entertainment industry in our country and the increasing emphasis on violent and sexually exploitative programs.

• We are concerned about the alarming amount of violence which occurs in American families each year, particularly the high incidence of child, spousal, and elder abuse.

• We are concerned about the prevalence of drug and substance abuse in our country, particularly among young people.

CWA GOALS

• We would like to see dignity and human rights restored to those who have lost their opportunities for self-determination.

• We would like to see the family restored to a place of prominence in society.

• We would like to see laws passed to protect the unborn.

- We would like to see the quality of education in public schools restored to a level of world prominence.
- We would like to see a balanced presentation of creation and evolution in public schools.
- We would like to see the religious heritage of our country presented without bias in public school classrooms and textbooks.
- We would like to see the preservation of religious freedoms as provided in the United States Constitution.
- We would like to see the United States deploy the strongest national defense system in the world as a deterrent to foreign aggression.
- We would like to see the reasonable appropriation of government monies and the fiscal responsibility to balance the federal budget.
- We would like to see society encourage young people to say "no" to premarital sex.
- We would like to see the strict enforcement of laws restricting the use and sale of pornography.
- We would like to see the entertainment industry become a more positive moral influence in society.
- We would like to see society address the physical and moral dangers of "alternative" lifestyles, promiscuous sexuality, and unnatural procreation.
- We would like to see more education intended to reduce family violence, especially the sexual abuse of children.
- We would like to see a dramatic reduction in drug and substance abuse, especially among young people.

KEY 16 PRAYER LIST

"I urge . . . that requests, prayers, intercession and thanksgiving be made for . . . all those in authority." (1 Tim. 2:1, 2)

U.S. GOVERNMENT

PRESIDENT_____ 1600 Pennsylvania Avenue
                                       Washington, D.C. 20500
                                       (202) 456-7639

CONGRESS
  Senate
    Senator _____ Senate Office Building
       _____ Washington, D.C. 20510
       Tel. No.   D.C.   Local

    Senator _____ Senate Office Building
       _____ Washington, D.C. 20510
       Tel. No.   D.C.   Local

  House of Representatives

    Congressman _____ House Office Building
       _____ Washington, D.C. 20515
       Tel. No.   D.C.

SUPREME COURT

Harry A. Blackmun	Thurgood Marshall	Antonin Scalia
William J. Brennan	Sandra D. O'Connor	John P. Stevens
Anthony Kennedy	William H. Rehnquist	Byron R. White

STATE GOVERNMENT

Governor _____

Legislature
  (State) Senator _____
                                Capitol Office
              District #_____ _____
                                  Local
  (State) Representative or
  Assemblyman _____
                                  Capitol Office
              District #_____ _____
                                    Local

Contact your local Registrar of Voters for the names of all your representatives and their district numbers. Pray for these by name each day. The people who fill these offices strongly influence the decisions that affect our families and our nation. They need prayers for divine guidance as they vote on important issues.

Concerned Women for America
P.O. Box 65453 • Washington, D.C. 20035–5453

1. Set aside a specific time for prayer each day.

2. Fill in Key 16 form with the names, addresses, and phone numbers. Remember to pray for them regularly.

3. Seek to educate yourself on moral issues.

4. Learn God's principles and the biblical basis for your stand on moral issues.

5. Become aware of current events and issues in your community, state, and nation that involve specific action. The *CWA Newsletter* gives vital information on national morality. We encourage you to read it on a regular basis.

6. Become involved in community programs that support your stand on moral issues.

7. Remember to pray for the specific prayer alerts given in the monthly *CWA News* from the national office and to participate in any action alerts that become necessary.

8. Prayerfully consider participation in CWA's "535" Program. (Information available on request.)

*Remember to pray for those who must make decisions in the CWA offices. Especially uphold our attorneys who research and represent our cases.

- -

We suggest you use the space below to write in the names of your local elected officials and pray for them also.

Mayor _____

County Supervisor _____

City Councilman _____

District Attorney _____

School Board Member _____

Sheriff _____

Dear Friend,

Over the years many people have confided in me about problems they have had in their prayer life. They have reported having no consistency, no power, and no real intimacy with God.

At Concerned Women for America, we have developed a unique prayer devotional entitled Strength For The Coming Days. *Using the Lord's Prayer as our guide, we have produced a systematic and powerful method of praying Scripture back to the Lord.*

By using the easy-to-follow pattern of scriptural prayer, you will cultivate your personal communication with Him and strengthen your walk with the Lord.

Strength For The Coming Days *delivers exactly what it says—real Strength For The Coming Days.*

The only way you may obtain your copy of Strength For The Coming Days *is by sending* **$9.95 to**
> **Concerned Women for America**
> **P.O. Box 65453**
> **Washington, D.C. 20035**

Or you may wish to call us at **800-458-8797** *to obtain your copy.*

By the way, **Strength for the Coming Days** *also makes a thoughtful gift for someone you love.*

Thank you,

Beverly LaHaye